Single Women –

Alive and Well!

edited by Dianne Lorang and Ann E. Byrnes

foreword by Gail E. Parsons, R.N., M.A.

SINGLE WOMEN – ALIVE AND WELL!
edited by Dianne Lorang and Ann E. Byrnes

Any correspondence with the individual authors should be directed to the editors. For information: The Write Help, LLC, 5743 South Prince St. PMB 2470 Littleton, CO 80120; Voice: (303) 738-0102; www.thewritehelp.net.

This book is printed on acid free paper.

Publisher's Cataloging-in-Publication
(Provided by Quality Books, Inc.)

Single women-- alive and well! / edited by Dianne Lorang
    and Ann E. Byrnes ; foreword by Gail E. Parsons. – 2nd
    ed.
        p. cm.
        Includes index.
        LCCN 00-093300
        ISBN 0-7596-0104-6

    1. Single women--Conduct of life. 2. Single women--
Psychology.   I. Lorang, Dianne II. Byrnes, Ann E.

HQ800.2.S56 2001   646.7'0086'52
                                        QBI01-700018

1stBooks-rev. 3/11/02

To Shelli, who liked me for myself, but more importantly, liked herself.

– Dianne Lorang

To brave and unnoticed women
who lay their hand on the shoulder of solitude,
finding there, within themselves,
survival, independence, and fulfillment—
the best of rewards.

– Ann E. Byrnes

Table of Contents

Acknowledgements

I couldn't be happier writing this part, as though I were writing my acceptance speech for the Academy Awards for best original screenplay. There are too many people to thank, but I will try. If I have forgotten anyone, please accept my apologies ahead of time and know you have my gratitude.

First, my co-editor, Ann E. Byrnes, for her friendship, insight, diligence, and enthusiasm, and believing in this project enough to work for free until it hits the bestseller list. Second, the subjects of my stories in this book, for they graciously gave me their permission to write about them, correcting any errors in the details of their lives, and honestly telling me when I had "gone too far." Third, the other writers of the stories, the one poem, and the Foreword (a work of love from Gail E. Parsons, R.N., M.A.).

Next, I must thank two very special clients who have not only advised me but inspired me: Lois Tschetter Hjelmstad, speaker and author of *Fine Black Lines: Reflections on Facing Cancer, Fear and Loneliness* (Mulberry Hill Press, 1993) and Willie Ripple, author of *The What Do I Do?*® series of party-planning books (Oakbrook Publishing House). And I can't forget those who have offered their services at a discount: Diane Young of Office Elves, Valerie Spagnolie, and Susan K. Bouse, Ph.D.

Other friends, co-workers, and authors who have encouraged me along the way are Cindy Rold, Jody Rein, Ann Mohin, Pam King, Sandra Bond, Cyndie Chandler, and Leslie Koffler. The rest of you know who you are. You've been there for me through thick and thin, listening to my whining, wiping my tears, sharing my laughter, and giving me hugs. You are all my family and no matter what, I know I am loved because of you.

Of course, I have a real clan and must thank them, for not only have they supported me emotionally, but been patient with me when I was tired, frustrated, and, frankly, putting my day job on hold much of the time while working on this book. My husband, Mike, who is cooking a fabulous dinner right now, wears his Birkenstock shoes as easily as his Harley Davidson motorcycle boots, and really does understand and appreciate this project. My daughter, Liz, for her encouragement and gratis typing and stuffing envelopes. My son, Bart, my daughter, Michelle,

Dianne Lorang and Ann E. Byrnes

and her husband, Paul, for being the excellent people they are—I am constantly amazed at their abilities!

I want to thank my parents, who still endure my ups and downs because they know I'm a writer-type, and my siblings and their mates and nieces and nephews…you have all taught me so much about kindness, joy, peace…as well as added to my creative life. My extended family, near and far. Then there are all the good folks in my husband's family, especially my in-laws who are the best—if they weren't, would I have taken my mother-in-law to Ireland for her seventy-fifth birthday last year?

Last, I thank my grandma who is ninety-six years old this year, still living in the house where my mother was a teenager, and who has shared more wisdom with me in the little time I get to spend with her than all the college professors, preachers, and psychiatrists I've known, put together. When I asked her what her secret was, why she didn't have any aches and pains, she looked me in the eye, even though she is legally blind, and said, "I don't hold any grudges." Thank you, Grandma. Thank you.

– Dianne Lorang

Foreword

As I read the stories in *Single Women – Alive and Well!*, I think about the importance of the individuation process in each of our lives—that process of finding out who we are as individuals. The psychiatrist Carl Jung spoke of this at length in his writings. The need for us to go on such a journey of self-discovery is especially evident at mid-life, he says. But it can happen at any time, as long as it does. If we avoid who we really are and what our true longings are, we stagnate, we die inside. We may even become bitter "grumpy old women."

The women in *Single Women – Alive and Well!* are in the midst of this important journey, for it never ends once it has begun. Once they have shed their old modes of transportation, they will find better and better ways to move through life. They may not go fast or by first class, but they will be content with the road they have chosen, even if they have to change directions several times to find their way. Throughout their wanderings, much as the heroines of great legends, they display courage, creativity, and endurance.

The writers in *Single Women – Alive and Well!*, whether they are single now or not, realize that it has been vital for each of them to uncover their talents, dreams, and ambitions. As we come to know who we are—including our feelings, desires, and abilities—our self-esteem grows, and we know what really matters is love. Not the romantic kind we used to think would fulfill us, although it certainly can be a wonderful part of life, but a love of self that allows us to love others.

It is this kind of love with which we do not just the big things in life for ourselves and others, but the small things as well. It may be cleaning out a closet or buying a new sweater. It may be calling a friend to have lunch or go to a movie. It may be writing a poem or writing in a journal. It may simply be showing up for work and giving it your all, or deciding to change careers. It may be forgiving the people in our lives who have hurt us the most. It is always about forgiving ourselves. Ultimately, the love we give cannot help but come back to us, in a way we never imagined before we packed our bags and kicked the dust off the feet of our old lives.

Single Women – Alive and Well! only gives us a glimpse of what can happen once a woman starts on her personal journey into self-knowledge.

Dianne Lorang and Ann E. Byrnes

The stories included here represent just small pieces of the writers' lives, yet critical parts showing they have "slain their dragons" and then shared their experiences with the world, not caring what other people think, only that they think for themselves. We are in danger as women, as individuals, and therefore as a society when we allow others to do our thinking for us. We must not just walk to the "beat of a different drummer," but find our own beat, even if we have no drummer.

– Gail E. Parsons, R.N., M.A., CACII
Contract Therapist, Outpatient Facilities
Englewood, Colorado

Introduction

The stories told in this book are those of single women who have helped me become the independent person I am today. Not financially or emotionally, but in thought and desire, in life goals and inner strength, which I believe come from a Higher Power, and should not come from another person, although other people are essential for our well-being. Even "significant others" can give us an extra boost. But they should never be our "significance."

Ironically, I am not a single woman myself, nor have I ever really been one in the conventional sense of the term. I was engaged at eighteen, married at nineteen, and at forty-seven, have been married to the same man for more than twenty-seven years. I have three grown children, all living close to us, one son-in-law, a nice home in the suburbs, but no pets. In that way, as in many others you will discover, I am not a typical (if there is one) married middle-class woman in mid-life. Still, you may wonder why I am compiling a book of stories about and by single women.

I've always been fascinated by, if not envious of, single women. Not the ones who moan and complain about their lonely lives, but the ones who are strong and happy on their own, having fought the social structure of our society to not just survive, but to thrive. How free they must be to choose their own path and make their own decisions, from financial to what TV shows to watch to what kind of house to live in, and where, and what church to go to, if any. How nice it must be to know you've made it on your own and "done it your way."

Don't get me wrong. I don't have a man who insists on ruling his castle. Not only is he sweet and funny, but a good father who has recently been pitching in more around the house. I'm downright lucky, some might be thinking, and yes, they may be right to think it, except they don't know that for most of our married life, I did everything but earn the paycheck. In short, they don't know me, and they don't know my story. They don't know why I got married, how I've stayed married, or what personal struggles I've had along the way.

Even I don't completely understand "me" or my marriage. I know that I don't take it for granted. Neither do I consider it "made in heaven" as more than one person has called it. My children would laugh at that, having lived through the ups and downs that are normal in any long-term relationship. And they aren't even aware of all the bad things; neither do they know all the good.

One of the best things, evident I hope to all those around me, is my personal growth as a separate entity from my husband. It was something that had to happen not just for the marriage to continue, but for me to live, literally. I was suffocating, dying inside. By the time I had been married a decade, the person I had started to become in my teen years was barely a memory.

I began writing way back then, and again when my children were very small, even getting published on my first venture out into the vast world beyond my domestic life. Yet there was something missing, something basic, which I assumed I could only find by returning to college, which I eventually did in my thirties. But that was not the beginning for me, nor was it the answer. It was simply part of my transformation.

I, like many other women, had made the error of making my husband the center of my existence. So one of the hardest challenges of my married life turned into one of my biggest blessings. In a time and place when most husbands came home every night to a hot meal on the table, and mowed the lawn and shoveled the snow (which can be a nine-month ordeal in Montana where we lived), my husband traveled the world on business, often leaving me alone to fend for myself and three little kids.

Mine was a lonely life, and I found the need for socializing in the evening outside the usual realm of Bible studies, choir practice, and the occasional baby shower. I needed friendship that was not based on a shared status as much as shared circumstances, of being on my own most of the time.

So I was drawn to single women who were as needy as I for companionship in what seemed like a world of couples. Some of my newfound friends had more of a "life" than I did, for people would invite them places, not thinking they'd be busy with domestic bliss. If I went anywhere without my husband, to anything unplanned by the usual social trappings of the time, I did the phoning.

And so it began. My finding myself without having to leave my life behind. It was simply a matter of balance, of not getting too hung up on thinking the grass was greener. On seeing the truth, being aware of reality, loving my children, remembering my commitment to my husband, but truly and deeply caring for myself like I never had, ever before.

I had been raised to be a homemaker, a caretaker, a helpmate to my husband, from a fundamentalist Christian perspective. I had taken care of my brother, though he was older than I, when our parents were divorced. I then helped my mother raise my two younger stepsisters and my baby half-sister when she remarried. No wonder I got married young. It was an easy transition. It was an easier life.

I thought I would finish college before starting a family, but it was to be the other way around because we started moving and I followed my man, putting down shallower and shallower roots with each new dwelling. And other things happened, having to do with life and death, family tragedy. I was still so young and living in the fast lane, I called it, ahead of schedule, knowing I would still be young as an empty-nester, which I am today.

All of which contributed to my need for an identity of my own. It hadn't been my one and only dream to get married and have a family and a nice home. I had goals, ambitions, even some brains and musical talent along with my way with words, all, it seemed, getting trampled by duty and difficult unpaid work. I was getting nowhere fast while my husband was progressing and my children were growing. I, as I've said, was dying.

Yet I didn't choose to run, though I thought a lot about it. I had worked too hard for the family I had. Besides, I had no real reason to go, so I stayed, knowing things would eventually have to change. Little did I know that I would do the majority of the changing, from a girl who allowed life to carry her on its coattails, to a woman who took life in her own hands, self-determining what she wanted and how to go about getting it, without upsetting the boat too much.

But I'm boring you, for I'm telling my story in generalities, and should save some of the tidbits for later in the book. Suffice to say that although I feel they are important enough to share with the world, they are not as significant as what the future holds. Thanks to the millions of women who have challenged the odds by not staying at home where they were told they "belonged," or in the hospitals behind a nursing station, or in front of a blackboard, or behind a secretary's desk in front of a closed door.

Some remained married, but many never got married or had to leave their partners to find true fulfillment. They decided, "I don't need a man to be happy." That doesn't mean they haven't found happiness with a man since then, but they haven't become dependent, saying, "I don't know how I'd live without him!"

Dianne Lorang and Ann E. Byrnes

My co-editor, Ann E. Byrnes, is one of these women. I met her years ago when I started on this book. We worked closely together on her first book, through her ups and downs as a single mother trying to make ends meet, trying to make sense of a troubled relationship. I don't believe she had unrealistic expectations, though, for she had been single ten years before her first marriage and another six before meeting her present partner. Her stories are in this book.

Other single women I have known are here, too, some in their own words, some in mine. Even those whose stories are not here helped me— they are in my heart, imprinted on my soul. I would not have made it without them and their support. I would not be who I am today. I would be depressed, or angry, or lonely, only associating with other unhappy women like I was before I realized it was totally up to me to change that.

You see, it wasn't my circumstances as much as it was my attitude. When I finally saw that I had choices, I began making them. When I learned I would be just fine on my own should my marriage, for some reason, end, that's when I started this book...

– Dianne Lorang

After a While

After a while you learn the subtle difference
    between holding a hand and chaining a soul
And you learn that love doesn't mean leaning
    and company doesn't mean security
And you begin to learn that kisses aren't contracts
    and presents aren't promises
And you begin to accept your defeats
    with your head up and your eyes ahead
    with the grace of a woman, not the grief of a child
And you learn to build all your roads on today
    because tomorrow's ground is too uncertain for plans
    and futures have a way of falling down in mid-flight.
After a while you learn that even sunshine burns
    if you get too much.
So you plant your own garden and decorate your own soul
    instead of waiting for someone to bring you flowers.
And you learn that you really can endure
    that you really are strong
    and you really do have worth
And you learn and you learn
    with every good-bye you learn...

– Veronica A. Shoffstall

The Lavender Dress
by Dianne Lorang

I am seven years old, or maybe eight by now. I am standing on the top cement stair of the entrance to our basement apartment. The address is six-hundred-something and a half. The house is dusty pink with a covered front porch. Right next door, on the corner, in a two-story white house with green shutters, lives a doctor with his wife and four children. Sometimes, my older brother and I go over there at night while the doctor reads out loud from *Pilgrim's Progress*, John Bunyan's classic story about Christian's journey to the Celestial City.

Across from the doctor and us is a dark brown house that has been turned into a corner grocery store. The man who runs it along with his wife is named Archie. No kidding. (I see him twenty or thirty years later at a funeral, and he reintroduces himself to me.) Archie doesn't know that I secretly dig into my mother's purse, down to the very bottom, to find pennies to buy candy from him. I feel a bit guilty, but not as bad as I was made to feel when I stole a whole chocolate bar from the little grocery store across from my father's apartment in our old town.

That wasn't that long ago, but it seems like it now. We have moved an eight-hour train ride from where I was born, where my grandparents live, where I went to kindergarten, starting in the middle of the year, and first grade, and half of second grade. Where I watched John Glenn orbit the earth in the teachers' lounge with my brother. We were the only students there because we had sack lunches. All the other kids went home for lunch. We were staying with our grandparents across town and got rides to school.

At least I didn't have to skirt around the red ants in the dirt path anymore, even though they were probably hibernating then if that's what ants do. I cried on that path, alone, on my way to school one day. I didn't know I could go off the path to get around the anthill. I was wearing one of those taffeta-like pastel-colored dresses we little girls still wore in the early 1960s, complete with buckle dress shoes and lace-top anklets. Someone must have come along and taken me by the hand. I don't know who.

The details of my early years are sketchy. "They were traumatic," my mother would explain to me later, without telling me what was so traumatic about them. Did my father beat me? Or worse? Did he beat my brother, my mother? Is it just my imagination, or did he leave my brother and me in the back seat of our green Packard while he drank away the night at a bar?

I remember my grandparents helping my mother pack up, in the middle of winter, and driving us to another town so my mom could go back to college, even though there was a college where we moved from. I think she wanted to get away from my father, far away. And it was far in those days, before the Interstate went in. So our father never came to visit us in our new home.

It is summer, the day I am standing on the top step of our basement apartment, the perfect weather time in Montana, when there aren't forest fires. I must have a babysitter in the apartment. My mother doesn't leave us alone at this point, even though my brother is ten. Probably because he can't control me. But for some reason, I am not misbehaving today. I am just standing on the top stair, waiting, watching. Even though it is here that a spider bit me on the knee that spring, and I howled and howled until someone came running.

It is a Saturday and my mother has gone away, by herself, for the whole afternoon. It isn't like her. She is always with us when she isn't at school. She couldn't have gone far without a car. And I know she'll be home soon. I hope she'll be home soon. I stand there looking past the white house with green shutters, past the brown grocer's, down toward the park one and a half blocks away where we sometimes go on our bikes to race up and over the grass-covered hills.

Then she appears. Walking so tall in high heels I've never seen before. So trim in a belted, full-skirted, cotton lavender dress that she must have bought today. She could be singing, the way she almost bounces up the street to our sidewalk. She is smiling, like I haven't seen her smile in months, maybe a year. Her brown short hair stands still in the breeze, the way it does when it has been freshly washed, set, and sprayed.

In one afternoon, something has changed. My mother has been transformed, as if doing something little, like taking some money she had saved from her meager support and treating herself special, could make such a difference. She deserves it, but I didn't know then what she had really gone through. My father had left her for another woman. She had wanted to drive her car, the one she had before the divorce, into oncoming traffic.

"But I didn't because of you and your brother," she would tell me.

2

That same summer, I see my father for the last time before I am grown. It is back at my grandparents' house where I'm visiting before school starts. He has come over and must have upset me. I remember him crouching in front of the big maple tree on the farthest corner of the lot, past the four apple trees, under the power pole. I can see him crying as I back away, then turn and run back to the little white house with red trim where my grandma still lives today, at ninety-six.

Apparently, I had learned to live without my father the same way my mother had, and life must have been better without him, for we were happy, the three of us, for the short time we lived in that basement apartment, before my mother remarried and gave me two younger stepsisters and a new baby half-sister.

Mom was usually happy after that, as long as she had some time for herself in the midst of taking care of all of us and the house, sewing, and wallpapering, and putting together Christmas baskets for friends. It became a good life, more or less, and it all started that summer day when Mom went to town and bought a lavender dress.

Just One American Beauty Rose
by Marilyn Farber Jacobs

The crash woke me. Sitting up, I looked around. In the dim light coming through the window, I saw my tall glass bud vase broken on the floor. My cat must have been admiring the red American Beauty rose I'd received that evening. "Oh, Candy," I sighed. "Your curiosity has done it again." I switched on the lamp, went to the hall closet, and took out the broom and dustpan.

"Brrrr. It's still cold." I remembered how I'd shivered outside earlier while waiting for the WALK sign, my breaths forming little clouds in front of me. Three cab drivers stopped and almost in unison started tapping their fingers on their steering wheels, feet no doubt poised above accelerators, anticipating the maneuver around Columbus Circle. I crossed the street and headed uptown, walking along Central Park.

With my black hat covering my head, I buried my chin in my black scarf, hunching up my shoulders, hands in my pockets. My black windbreaker had a Burberry beige, white, red, and black plaid fabric on its cuffs and collar. The red plush pile lining, neither detachable nor visible, kept me warm. My pants and walking shoes, too, were black...*the* New York color, especially in winter. "It's such a thrifty idea," I reasoned. "If everything I buy is black, everything matches."

Very few people were out in the strong wind. Mid-February in New York City is usually like this. "But I'm here," I mused, "where I decided to move, so I'll just have to get used to the cold."

My friend Jeffrey had e-mailed me from Florida where he'd spent the morning on a beach. *Come on down*, he wrote. *I saw your weather report, and you have my sympathy!*

I kept up an even pace. "Heel, toe, heel toe," I said out loud, concentrating on getting the most out of my walk, like the book I was reading had instructed. My large black handbag, the size leftover from years of carrying a diaper bag, rested easy on my shoulder. But it got in the way of swinging my left arm, so I just did the best that I could. "This," I thought, "is *real* exercise."

I crossed over at 66th Street and continued up Central Park West. Twice, as I walked north, I had to stop for the light, breaking my rhythm.

I'd eaten at a nice Italian restaurant on Columbus Avenue several times before. A friend had recommended it. "I'll go there tonight," I thought, raising my eyebrows. "I'll treat myself to capellini with tomato sauce and capers." I was feeling good, free, emancipated from a marriage that had been going nowhere.

I marched past apartment buildings with doctors' offices on the ground floors, signs advertising their specialty. A young deliveryman stood outside a deli, rocking back and forth to keep warm. An elderly man was walking his dog. But mostly I scanned the architecture, sometimes craning my head to see it. A few buildings featured art deco designs, dating them back to the 1940s.

I rounded the corner and walked south on Columbus Avenue, almost always filled with people. You can window shop, or buy clothing and makeup in airy, well lit, non-intimidating boutiques, often open at night, with young attractive twenty-something salesmen and women. On warm days and nights, you can eat outside and watch passersby, couples holding hands.

Even though it was not yet 6:00, the official start of the dinner hour, a Chinese restaurant was already half filled. I paused long enough to look at its taped-up menu, but still wanted pasta.

A man and woman walked into the next restaurant with their little boy. Its menu read in big bold letters, FAMILY STYLE PLATTERS. "I'll bring my grandchildren here sometime," I fantasized, and kept going.

When I reached the Italian restaurant, I went inside to find almost all the tables taken, the conversations melding into a loud buzz. I smiled at the host, "Table for one, please."

"Madame," he said, "I cannot accommodate 'one' this evening, we have no table for you." He then turned to the next woman and asked, "Table for two?"

"Really?" I asked. He glanced at me but did not answer. I'd been dismissed. "Did he reject me because I was alone?" I wondered. It *was* Valentine's Evening.

It had happened to me before, several times. The first time I had felt devastated. Left out. Discarded. Invisible. I felt a slow anger rising. "I'll call the owner tomorrow," I thought. "Tonight is too perfect to throw away."

There are enough restaurants in this area, I knew I'd find another one quickly, maybe a quieter one. As I walked along, a little faster now, I told

6

myself I would never go back there. The other times I'd been alone, they'd been happy to feed me, but a single woman, on this night...

I remembered going into almost vacant restaurants other times where I'd been led to an undesirable table, near the kitchen. I would gesture towards a better location and say I wanted to sit there. They usually moved me, but if they wouldn't, I'd leave and go elsewhere. I figured, "It's my money and I want to feel comfortable, respected, and taken care of. I want to feel that way *all* the time."

I continued down Columbus Avenue, crossed the street, and stopped at a restaurant I'd never noticed before, for good reason. A food market adorned its front with permanent though empty bins and shelves. An awning projected out over those. Polished wood paneling framed a large glass window, beckoning me to peek in.

An arrangement of large red shrimp flowers and exotic leaves sat on the bar. The lighting was set at a comfortable glow, making the place look warm and inviting. Scanning the menu by the door, I saw *sea bass*. My mouth watered. The prices were a bit high, but I peered in again. Only a few tables were taken. I went inside.

The hostess was wearing a black dress with a red jacket, shoulders squared with pads, her black hair styled in a pageboy. She sat me at a table for two. One side wall was brick, the other painted white. There were etchings of buildings and New York City scenes in black frames. The tables had white linen cloths, and the glasses and flatware had an upscale look, making me feel special, showing promise that I would be treated well. So many times I'd been to a restaurant where the food was good, but the ambiance was not. I sat back, content and hopeful.

The servers and busboys were in clean, white, starched uniforms, and they were smiling. My waitress told me the specials. I started with a glass of white zinfandel wine. I like sweet wines. It came in a generous round shaped goblet with a delicate stem. "Elegant!" I whispered.

My salad combined the flavors of apples, skinny red onion slices, lettuces, and goat cheese with balsamic dressing. So far, I rated the restaurant as excellent. The service was polite, and not rushed. The busboy kept my water glass filled. I like lots of water. I did have to ask a second time for a slice of lemon, hardly a major catastrophe.

The kitchen prepared my sea bass as requested, grilled rather than sautéed, butter sauce on the side. There were mashed potatoes with herbs, baby carrots mixed with sweet red peppers, and a sprig of broccoli with a delicious white sauce. I ate slowly, leaving a small amount on my plate, too full to order dessert. I declined coffee, feeling completely satisfied.

My watch read 6:45. I paid the check, leaving a generous tip. The restaurant was full now, and there were about two dozen people waiting. Most were in casual dress but neat looking. At that moment, the waitress came over and put one long stemmed American Beauty rose wrapped in cellophane on my table. "This is for *you*, Madame," she said.

"Thank you, it's beautiful. And so thoughtful." I noted that not every female patron had received such a gift.

I thanked the hostess for the rose and put the restaurant's card in my purse. "I'll definitely be back," I told her. "Next time, I'll bring friends." I walked south toward my apartment building, smiling all the way home.

Fear in Seville
by Jan Neville

There I was, an American woman alone, walking briskly off to see a bullfight in Seville. I was scared but determined. I had lived too long to pass up this chance. To keep up my resolve, I repeated "Tor-re-a-dor-a tum-te-tum-te-tum," the song from the opera *Carmen,* over and over again in my head, my steps keeping time to the music as I walked. Soon, I had gone the ten blocks to the visitors' center by the cathedral.

I don't read or speak Spanish, but I could understand the posters with the picture of the bull and bullfighter and the number of the day. "Where is the bullfight?" I asked.

The lady behind the counter replied, "They sell tickets at the box office which opens at noon at the Plaza De Toros De Sevilla. You're not alone, are you?"

I smiled, reassuring both her and myself. She dutifully marked directions for me on a city map. "How far?" I asked. "Can I walk?"

She nodded "yes," but as I turned, I heard a whispered "not good."

"Does anyone want to go to the bullfight?" I had queried my fellow Arts and Communication Conference attendees.

"Why do you want to see a poor defenseless bull get killed? It's inhumane!" replied the lady from Singapore.

"But the bull is not wasted," I told her. "It is food for the poor."

"I saw a bullfight in Mexico City and it was really boring," said a Californian.

"Oh, these bullfights in Seville are the minor leagues. If you really want to see a good bullfight, Madrid is the place," came the verdict from an American male.

Nobody wanted to go, and they thought it strange that I did. But my philosophy is that in one world, we must understand all cultures, by experiencing them as much as we can.

It was my last day in Spain, the end of an extended tour after an international conference. I had only today on my own to do what I wanted. *See a bullfight, their national sport*, I had written in my notebook. I had seen bullfights in movies and pictures, and heard about the fiasco bullfight during the Gold Rush near Cripple Creek, Colorado, close to where I live.

Now was my chance to experience one in the center of their origin. Either I went alone or not at all. A big dilemma for a long-time widowed school librarian who believed in "safety in numbers." I remembered other trips when I had let my fear of going alone overcome my desire to see all that a place had to offer.

"Yes, you must go," I told myself. "Quit expecting others to change their minds. Quit wasting time. Go. Now. Before you lose your nerve. Tor-re-a-dor-a..."

I was off to the box office. Time, destination, and a plan had strengthened my courage. But the street on the way was deserted. I saw no people standing in lines at the plaza, and began to wonder if I was in the right place.

"What am I doing here?" I thought. "Tor-re-a-dor-a..." As I moved along the outside wall of what I assumed to be the arena, I discovered an open door with a counter inside. Timidly I asked, "Tickets to the bullfight?"

The man answered, "Si," as he got up from his desk and came to the counter. He showed me the arena seating chart. Using a mixture of English, Spanish, and pantomime, we discussed the pricing. He explained the most expensive seats had a roof while the sun was in your eyes in the cheapest seats.

"No sun. No roof," I said. "In between."

"How many?"

"One, just me."

The man looked at the other two men in the office, then back at me. "You? Alone?"

"Yes." I smiled as I pointed with one finger at myself. I realized numbers in a different language are confusing, but this man seemed more uneasy than usual.

One of the other men stepped forward and pulled a ticket out. I saw a look of relief come over the first man as we exchanged ticket and money.

My seat was on the left of the aisle. I noticed that three seats stayed empty across the aisle as well as next to me. The same three seats in the two rows behind me and below me remained unoccupied, on both sides of the aisle. An older man sat a few steps down on the dividing walkway.

There I was, in a mass of humanity in an arena filled with people, sitting by myself. It was like being on an island, others close by, but not elbow to elbow. At first I thought, "Oh, it's early. Others will come in later."

As vendors came by, they sat for a while with the older man. Other men came—watching, discussing, laughing, smiling, joking, drinking, but not getting drunk. Then they moved on.

When I realized I could plainly see the box office and its three attendants, I knew that the supervisor had picked a seat where I would be easy to watch (in case I got hysterical over the proceedings, or even fainted). They could also watch for pickpockets.

They were there if I needed them, but respected my decision, perhaps even admired my guts for wanting to see a bullfight on my own.

I interpreted their body language—their pointing, laughing, and smiles were not about me but about the old man, their boss, "baby-sitting" me. I suddenly felt as safe as in a Safeway back home.

A vendor came by shouting, "Prograina de Toros."

"English," I shouted back. He handed me one for approximately two dollars. At first I was worried he hadn't understood, wondering how he picked out an English one so quickly. Then I discovered the English version was at the beginning of the booklet followed by French, German, Spanish, Dutch, Italian, and Japanese.

It was filled with colorful pictures plus six pages which explained the order and procedure of the whole bullfight. I read that the president conducts the *corrida* with the assistance of an assessor, usually a retired *torero*, and an expert veterinary surgeon. The health department is underneath the arena seats, to inspect the meat.

The first *matador* of the day, dressed in pink satin, strutted into the ring. He faced the bull, twirling his cape with ritualistic precision. Between my watching the event on the field and reading the description in the program, the first bullfight was over quickly. I didn't even have time to get emotionally involved.

From the movies, I expected a bloody mess, the bull to be dragged around and around the stadium. Instead, he was off the field within one minute, hooked onto a rack pulled by two horses, the sand over the area where he had fallen raked clean. The audience applauded but did not seem like they were there for the violence. Rather, they exalted the bull for his part in facing the man bravely.

When the second matador walked into the ring, I noted his hesitation immediately. The boss man below me turned and caught my eye as I shook my head "no" with a sad expression on my face.

I had seen the fear of that matador in his walk, his fate sealed in that minute. The bull also sensed his fear. Eventually, the president had to

11

signal an assistant to kill the bull, to the disgrace of the matador. He would possibly never perform again.

I thought of the fear I had faced in coming to the bullfight alone. The fact that, once I had made the decision, I kept moving forward purposefully and had achieved my goal. How if I had even flinched for one moment...

With relief, I joined the applause as the first matador returned to the ring.

He executed the third bullfight brilliantly. Slowly, hypnotically, he glided toward the bull, then back, teasing with his cape, moving in ever-closer, keeping eye contact with the beast, until the bull moved his head lower and lower, finally bowing to the matador.

To the crowd's delight, the matador reached out with his hand and rested it for a minute on the bull's head, his cape and sword in his other hand. Then he turned his back on the bull, his head held high, shoulders back. The crowd went wild. The matador looked to the president for permission to kill the bull.

Returning to the animal, he manipulated his cape and sword with finesse and completed the kill with speed and accuracy. The audience rose to their feet as one, waving their handkerchiefs. The matador bowed and proudly paraded around the ring as flowers, cigars, hats, and handkerchiefs fell in front of him, the feeling of triumph tremendous.

The day's entertainment was officially over. I watched the arena empty, trying to absorb not just what I felt, but how the two matadors must feel, one victorious, one disgraced.

A couple of children were out on the field. They had horns on a triangle. Their fathers watched and laughed while they imitated the matadors. "All cultures, all people," I thought, "have horns of dilemma."

I smiled, my head held high, shoulders back. "Tor-re-a-dor-a tum-te-tum-te-tum," I hummed out loud, knowing I had faced my fear in Seville.

Crossing Lost Trail
by Pat Wulle

It was 9:00 in the morning when I started north on I-15 in my seven-year-old Ford Escort. Pretty good planning as the Salt Lake City going-to-work traffic had thinned and I could enjoy the beautiful blue-skied early October day.

I'd been hesitant to embark on this trip and had found many excuses for postponing it. Yet I wanted to see my sister and her family, my brother and his wife, my ninety-one-year-old aunt[1] who is blind, and my favorite cousin, now alone. It would be good to see my husband's sisters, too. I've known them since childhood and we were friends long before we were in-laws.

Driving the 500 plus miles would be a challenge. Until my husband Freddie's death three years ago, my driving had been limited to the six miles back and forth to work, runs to the grocery store, and an occasional trip to the mall.

Since that time, I've learned to maneuver around Salt Lake City by back streets where the traffic is slow and sparse. In the summer, I've been able to coax grandkids into accompanying me on the 100-mile trip to the cabin.

My three sons worry about my driving, and I'm not really sure that they don't have good reason.

I didn't invite anyone to go with me on this excursion to Montana. My boys and their wives were working, and the grandkids were in school. But I couldn't quite silence the uneasy thought, "Can I handle this alone?"

It wasn't my driving or the aging car that was bothering me. As long as I had my checkbook and my VISA card, I could handle most emergencies. It was going home without my husband and best friend of forty-five years that upset me.

We had covered these same miles dozens of times in the thirty-five years since we had moved from Montana. First, there had been fun vacation trips with a carload of noisy boys and a dog or two, heading home to visit the grandparents and family and then on to Lake Ronan, our favorite fishing spot, the place we had spent our honeymoon many years ago.

---

[1] Editor Dianne Lorang's grandmother.

Next had come the dreaded trips when we rushed home at the news of sickness and then later, those trips where we watched our loved ones being put to rest.

After that, the trips weren't as frequent. The kids had grown up and didn't go as much. Sometimes it was just the two of us; sometimes we invited friends so we could show off the beautiful country we both loved.

Now I was making this trip all alone without Freddie who had always been there for me, loving me for what I was and not faulting me for what I wasn't. His acceptance had given me confidence and quelled my doubts.

I've been proud of myself for doing just fine as a widow. Proud to be a "tough old broad" who doesn't complain a lot and seldom asks for help. I've learned to remember the good times and forget the bad. Freddie and I had more than our share of both, and I have a myriad of wonderful memories.

I've searched out means of keeping my days busy. I leave the television on all night and find solace in books. I have conversations with Dazimae, my little scruffy dog (who bosses and bullies me, and doesn't really like me much). Anything to keep the ghosts from creeping in and cracking my veneer.

As I cruised along the freeway, I kept the radio playing, listening to an interesting talk show until the static drowned it out. After stopping in Tremonton, Utah, for a cup of coffee and a cinnamon roll, I found familiar voices on a "golden oldies" station.

I had informed my kids and my sister that I planned to drive only as far as Idaho Falls, where I'd spend the night and continue the trip the next day. But when I got there at 1:30 in the afternoon, I wasn't tired and felt pretty darned confident about my traveling capabilities.

So I decided to leave the freeway and take Highway 93 up over Lost Trail Pass through the Bitterroot Mountains. Outside of Roberts, Idaho, I noticed a sign saying something about Highway 93, but I wasn't quick enough to read the message. Anyway, whatever it said, the road wasn't closed, so I kept going.

I became nervous as I proceeded across the desert between Roberts and Salmon, Idaho—there were practically no cars. Maybe every fifteen minutes someone would pass me heading south.

Worse yet, the only radio stations coming in carried bad country music or "right-wing" talk, one equally as distasteful to me as the other. I would turn the radio off but the silence made me uneasy, so I would turn it back on.

If only I'd brought Dazimae along for company. Oh, well, Rush Limbaugh was better than nothing.

Reaching Salmon about 5:00, I found a coffee shop, sat in a booth, ordered a meal, and ate by myself. This was a big deal, something I hadn't been able to bring myself to do since Freddie had died.

Then more "firsts": I checked into a motel, went for a long walk in a strange town, bought myself a wine cooler and a box of Fiddle Faddle, and took them back to the motel to snack on as the television lulled me to sleep.

I woke up early, while it was still dark out. At breakfast, I found out that Highway 93 was under construction over Lost Trail Pass and would only be open at two-hour intervals. (That must have been what the sign outside of Roberts had tried to tell me.)

I left early enough to reach the start of construction before they closed the road, proceeding at the required 25 MPH up the steep winding highway towards Montana.

Dense evergreen forest dotted with orange tamarack appeared in the dawn as far as the eye could see. As the sun rose, reds and pinks gleamed behind the rugged Bitterroot peaks.

Each hairpin turn in the familiar road reminded me of other trips and other days...

A flip of the radio dial produced nothing—no Newt Gingrich sound-alikes, no whiney western music—nothing. I was suddenly terrified, feeling trapped in silence and isolation.

Other drivers had been shrewd enough to read the signs and follow other routes. Up here at the pass, I was alone.

Memories bombarded my brain, good and bad, unleashed by the silence after years of careful stifling.

Suddenly, all my confidence vanished, and I was overwhelmed by confusion.

I realized I was going home to a home that was no more. Most of the ones who had shared that world with me were gone and those that remained had lived their own lives.

Our lives no longer meshed.

How could I face the people of my past without Freddie, with his repertoire of jokes and ready "line of bull" that made folks laugh, that kept the conversations light and flowing. Freddie with his easy wit that could make me smile when I wanted to cry.

We were a team. I'd been the Abbott to his Costello, while he was the Gracie to my Burns. He was Ralph and I was Alice. What's one without the other? What good is the straight man without his clown?

"Who am I now?" I thought. I didn't know.

More than anything, I wanted to turn around, wind my little Ford up as fast as it would go, and head back to the safety of my tacky old trailer, my kids, and my dog.

But I couldn't—I'd said I'd be there. The distant past started to haunt me.

I told myself, "Remember the good stuff—just the good stuff—don't think about the bad times.

"If Freddie were only here to make me feel whole and help me pretend there'd been no times of pain and panic. If only the damned radio would work."

A lifetime of unshed tears began to wash down my face as I wallowed in an ocean of self-pity that my pride must have always kept at bay.

Yet I edged onward, down the pass to the past that had no future, afraid to interface with those who care, good people, people I love.

I was afraid of the awkward silences where feelings might creep in.

We were brought up to be strong. Love is always there but never spoken. We accept hugs with embarrassment but never initiate them. We're a tough bunch and proud of it. God forbid they find out I've been crying.

When I arrived at my sister's house at Stevensville, Montana, in the Bitteroot Valley, I was almost glad she wasn't home.

Not knowing what else to do, I drove the thirty miles to Missoula, Montana, still distraught and shaken. I'd worn my old walking shoes and forgotten to bring an extra pair. Maybe if I stopped at K-Mart to buy some new ones, I could pull myself together.

As I drove into the parking lot, a familiar old red pickup pulled in beside me and my sister got out.

"Hey, wouldn't you know we'd meet at K-Mart?" she joked. She had expected me to stay in Idaho Falls as planned and figured I would arrive later.

When I heard her voice and saw her grin, my world, my life, *all* was right. I *could* remember the good stuff and bury the rest. We laughed together. I was home.

My First Teacher
by Dianne Lorang

It is the mid-1970s. We are playing cards at Margie's house. Her youngest brother comes in so drunk, it takes both my husband and Margie's boyfriend to help him down the stairs to bed. No one seems alarmed or surprised. This is Montana, after all, where "men are men," and boys, well, boys drink.

This is also a home without parents. The father, my husband's uncle, killed himself seven years ago when Margie was a senior in high school. When her mother died from breast cancer last year, Margie came home to raise her two teenage brothers.

The three middle siblings have lives of their own. But Margie makes sure they all come home for holidays, insisting the six of them are still a family. She stuffs and roasts the turkey, having taught herself from the step-by-step instructions in her mother's tattered *Betty Crocker's Cookbook*. And Margie keeps a clean house. The dryer is always clanging with the sound of jeans.

Margie also works part-time as a desk clerk at the Ponderosa Motel so she can be home with the boys when they need her. She is as dedicated a guardian as they come. She doesn't let her boyfriend sleep over, she goes to parent-teacher conferences, and she never complains. Even when it would be so easy for her to chime in when I use her as a sounding board.

I am, you see, miserable, although I am practically a newlywed and only have prospects for a bright, bubbly future. I guess I expected married life to magically transform me into a happy person. But one thing is true: If a woman isn't happy before marriage, no amount of marital bliss can make her so. It would take me a long, long time to learn that. My first "teacher" would be Margie.

It is 1980. Margie had to say good-bye to her boyfriend because he wanted to get married and start a family. She decided that raising her brothers and being the family matriarch had fulfilled her needs that way. She is not bitter, but the same good-natured person she has always been.

I have yet to see her upset, even when she would be justified. But she's not a doormat. She doesn't let others tell her how to live her life, nor does she worry about what they think, like when they say, "Poor Margie, if she

17

could only find a man and settle down." They don't know that she is settled, and very happy.

She is now the receptionist in the town's one shopping mall's management office. She answers the phone with "Holiday Village, where good things happen." I always surprise her at the office when I am in town and we make plans for Sunday morning brunch, just the two of us. She is the big sister I never had. She is a good listener. She cares.

I am selfish and self-centered, thinking that I have no control over my life. Blaming my husband or my parents or anyone I can for my unhappiness. I don't understand, not yet anyway. But I have begun to write and Margie encourages me, telling me how talented I am.

It is the mid-1980s and I live in Colorado. Margie comes to visit me on her way to a business conference. She still works for Holiday Village. My husband is off on one of his many business trips.

I mind that very much and think if he really loved me, he wouldn't travel so much. I am not grateful for the fact that he supports me and our three young children.

I tell Margie all about the woes of married life, my fantasies about running away, how hard it is to be a stay-at-home mom, and how lucky she is. She doesn't lecture. She doesn't judge. She has faith in me, despite my bad attitude.

She never divulges what I share with her. She simply tells me about her boyfriends, who are fewer and farther apart as she has reached her mid-thirties.

I must confess that, even though I am unhappy, I think she would be happier if she were married. I am totally unaware, still, of her source, her strength, her secret. I don't think she knows she has one, it has come so naturally to her.

Perhaps she is right—she was the one woman for Elvis and since he died, there is no one for her. I think it is her way of gently getting nosy people off her back. I know she's not pining away for The King.

It is 1990 and I live back in Montana. I'm going to college. I think that if I get an education, I'll be happy. I have no specific plans of what to do with a degree, other than to write and get published more. I've had a couple successes.

I don't need to earn a living, although I'd like to be able to if it should come to that. I don't know if I can stay married to a man who doesn't make me happy like he's supposed to. He's forty, as is Margie, and I'm not getting any younger myself.

Margie has been promoted to mall manager (with only one year of college when she was eighteen). She has a hysterectomy to prevent cancer of the uterus. She buys the family home from her siblings. She is happier than ever, though working very hard.

I'm going through roller coaster life changes, and she's there for me whenever I need her. Because single women are more available to go out, most of my friends are single. The married women I know are boring, I think, or only go places with their husbands.

My husband isn't around much, and when he is, wants to stay home. It's the last thing I want to do. I think life would be better on my own. I can't wait for the kids to grow up.

It is the mid-1990s and I'm back in Colorado. My husband has been transferred, again. It will be our third time living here. We came for a short time as newlyweds before moving back to Montana twenty years ago.

My oldest child is grown and at college in the East. My two other children are teenagers and in high school. I have a job with a literary agent and should be happy. But I'm not. I want to edit more, or write more, or earn more, or have more friends, or go out more, or go out less. I don't know. I still haven't discovered how to be content.

We go home to Montana for a summer vacation. Margie drives out to my husband's folks' place in the country and we go for a walk, away from the 100 or so relatives gathered there for a family birthday party.

Margie still persists in telling me how much she admires me for going to college, everything I should want to hear. But I know the truth. I know I'm a failure and she's the success. I think it's because I'm married and she's not.

It's the last time we're truly, truly close. I don't know why. Maybe I need to break away from my husband's family somehow. I'm not yet ready to leave him physically, but emotionally, I'm gone.

I so desperately need a new start. I want to be like Margie, to be strong and independent, out on my own.

It is a new millennium. Margie just surprised us last night for my husband's fiftieth birthday party. I haven't seen her alone for years. We go out as a threesome to breakfast.

19

Dianne Lorang

I miss her, our times together. I don't think she knows her influence on me. How much I admire her. How I finally learned—after practically having a nervous breakdown, going through early menopause, and spending a lot on therapy—that I could be as happy being married as she is being single.

It's all a matter of attitude. It's learning to be content no matter what one's circumstances. She's always been the same regardless of life's events.

She has had a steady boyfriend for a few years now, yet they have no plans to get married or even live together. She likes her life just the way it is, although she's looking forward to retiring, as is my husband.

Me, I've only begun, but then it took me a long time to get started, to figure out what I needed as a person and then go after it. I wasted a lot of time wishing and waiting when I already had what so many single women wish and wait for.

We should all be thankful for what we *do* have, and live in the present. It is, pardon the pun, a gift, whatever package it comes wrapped in.

Embracing the Mundane
by Lana Book

It is 1977. Ginny and I are having coffee as seven children (four hers, three mine) run in and out, slamming the door behind them. The screen at the bottom of the door is separated from its molding, allowing the pesky midsummer flies easy entry. It is ten in the morning. The searing West Texas sun brings the thermometer outside the kitchen window to a record ninety degrees.

It is the kind of heat that drives a person to madness. A weatherworn silent madness. By three in the afternoon it will peak at a suffocating 110 degrees, at least. The swamp cooler on the top of the house groans as it tries to cool our flat-roofed track house.

Ginny and I kick off our shoes and enjoy the comfort of the cool tile floor. We remind me of one of those "before and after" photos, I the "before" and Ginny the "after." I feel transparent, as fragile most days as rice paper. If I were a stranger looking at us, I would see me, sallow and disheveled, with the stature of a rag doll.

In contrast, Ginny's emerging self-confidence is beginning to show in her straight posture and clear blue eyes. She has that glow of slow-burning embers about her. The kind you instinctively know is safe to warm up to without getting burned.

Last night's dried spaghetti dishes, and bowls with bits of concrete-hard oatmeal from breakfast, line the counter. Ginny offers to help. She washes, I dry. I listen, she talks. She tells me her twenty-year marriage ended in divorce two years ago.

"John used to call me his 'horizontal inspiration.' According to him, sex was the only area of our marriage where I didn't fail. It was a good fake. Beyond the first couple of years, the whole thing left me feeling as cold as neon.

"After years of emotional neglect and his domination over every aspect of my existence, I decided it was him or me.

"I had no idea how I would make it with four children to raise, no job skills, and only a vague memory of what it felt like to have any self-esteem. I just knew if I didn't do something, my soul would vaporize like pouring salt on a slug.

"I found a part-time newspaper route and enrolled in nursing school. Not that I ever wanted to be a nurse, but I could graduate in one year and save some money in the meantime.

"John opposed my every effort. Maybe he sensed what was really happening.

"I woke at four every morning, wrapped papers, completed my route, and was back home by six to get the kids ready for school. Then I would drop them off on my way to class."

Ginny and I know each other from church, and our children attend the same school, but we have never been what you would call real friends. She heard from the secretary at the rectory that I am getting a divorce and thought she would offer some support.

I used to watch her walk into church behind John, looking sad and defeated. I told myself then that I had a stable marriage. I would never be that miserable. I had felt smug and sorry for this woman I barely knew.

"What was the one thing that made you decide to end your marriage?" I ask her. "What was your breaking point?"

"It's going to sound ridiculous, but it was his lack of 'bathroom etiquette.'"

I start to laugh. I'm going to like this woman, I think.

"I know it seems insignificant compared to the big picture, but I couldn't stand going into the bathroom after John—stepping over wet towels and dirty boxer shorts on the floor. The smell around the toilet mixed with the sweetness of too much Old Spice cologne made me wretch.

"One morning after he left for work, I was cleaning around the shower drain and something in me just snapped. I sat down, right in the wet shower, and cried. I decided then that I couldn't stand cleaning up someone else's body hair from a steamy shower every morning for another twenty years or more.

"Especially when I got nothing in return. It was the ultimate indignity."

"I understand, I really do, Ginny. I can still see my mother on her hands and knees scrubbing the yellow ring around the base of the commode that left the linoleum permanently discolored."

"So tell me," Ginny asks, "did you have a breaking point, something that made you go right over the edge?"

"It was a similar experience, except my bathroom was a sanctuary. It was the one place I could retreat to behind a locked door and find some peace, early in the morning before anyone else was awake.

"One day, just as I got settled in the tub with water up to my neck, I heard a weak tap-tap-tap on the door, then David's voice: 'Honey, don't you want to come back to bed with David?' The fact that he always referred to himself in the third person should have sent up red flags years ago.

"'No, David, I don't,' I said with as much kindness as I could muster at five in the morning.

"Then came the inevitable: 'Ple-e-e-ase.'

"Enough was enough. 'Look, David,' I said. 'Call it weird, call it a spiritual thing, call it none of your damn business, better yet, call a taxi!'

"I think he was waiting for my permission to leave anyway. Our relationship had been deteriorating for more than a year. I had never denied David anything before, and when he left he said I never would again. So that was that."

But my story is just beginning. I want to know more about Ginny, how this woman who married when she was just sixteen, who never did anything without permission, who never managed her own money or held down a job, how she had faced the unknown.

Ginny says she survived her divorce by washing dishes. Not financial survival, but the "how do I get up and face the day?" kind of survival. The one thing that gave her comfort was to plunge her hands into hot soapy water.

Starting with the glasses, she would wash and dry them by hand, then hold them up to the window above her kitchen sink, catching the sun's light and warmth. Even dried egg yolk on plates and between fork tines became a medium for meditation as she watched it slowly melt, turning the water a creamy yellow.

Her greatest sense of self-accomplishment came while washing pots and pans, scrubbing and scouring through hard layers of black residue that had baked on over the years, reclaiming a part of herself as each original surface finally appeared.

"Seeing those dishes sparkle, seeing my reflection in something pure and tangible, gave me hope in the midst of chaos," she tells me. "It was the one thing I could accomplish every day that made me feel secure."

It is now 1997. Ginny has just returned from a world tour. Her children are grown and since she has invested her money wisely through the years, she can afford to travel. We are reminiscing about the last two decades. My daughter is listening. She wants to know how we survived it all. Ginny and I look at each other and smile.

Ginny says, "I remember one particularly grueling day of dealing with lawyers who showed no emotion and children who blamed me for everything. I gathered every dish, pot, and pan from the cabinets, even the good china from the hutch in the dining room, and I washed them over and over until my hands were cracked and bleeding. It was then I knew I would survive."

"We were there for each other," I say. "We must have come up with a hundred ways to disguise macaroni and cheese. We shopped together to save gas and share coupons, and watched each other's kids while we looked for jobs and worked.

"You should see how fast Ginny can roll a newspaper. I helped her paint her house and she helped me with car repairs. Do you remember when we tried to change the oil filter on my car?"

"Lord, what a mess!" Ginny laughs. "You should have seen us lying on our backs under that big Pontiac. We called it 'the tank.'"

"By the time we finished, that oil filter was a pathetic crumpled ball of metal. At least we had enough sense to drain the oil first!"

We wipe the tears of laughter from our eyes.

"You did good, Girlfriend," Ginny says. "Who knew back then that you would someday be living in an upscale townhouse and running your own business?"

"Well, I never would have guessed it twenty years ago. But my success was earned one step at a time, like a wound that heals slowly from the inside out."

We tell my daughter we rejoiced in each other's triumphs and supported each other when we failed. Just like we do now, we laughed, we cried, we talked.

Oh, we talked a lot in that old kitchen, watching kids run in and out—slamming the door every five minutes—swatting flies, and drinking coffee.

We tell my daughter we survived by embracing the familiar, even the mundane, by acknowledging our own courage and energy, by learning to enjoy the small things in life and not taking ourselves too seriously.

By reaching into the depths of our beings and awakening healing powers passed down for centuries, from woman to woman, friend to friend, and now mother to daughter...

Slaying Dragons
by CeLeste Lee

I wrestled the slide bar on the huge galvanized gate, pushed it open, then quickly closed it, securing the rope to tie it shut. Panting, I faced my enemy through the slats. He stared at me, and pulled back his lips to bare his huge white teeth. My heart was still racing when he bent his head to the ground and came up with a plug of near-dry grass.

"You can blame yourself for the condition of the grass!" I shouted, kicking dirt at his hooves. This was my second attempt to reconnect the irrigation pipes that had sprung apart from too much pressure. Pressure caused by a tiny frog lodged in the water release valve.

I knew my fear of large animals was irrational, but that didn't change it. I was stuck waiting for them to meander to the far end of the pasture. Thinking of the valuable minutes wasted, I pressed my cheek against the cold steel and watched my tears pool in the dry Texas dust at my feet.

"But is it progress to take my anger out on a horse rather than shake my fist at heaven?" I wonder. "By now, even God must be bored with my useless tirades and unanswered questions.

"There is so much to do. I could work twenty-four hours a day and never finish.

"This was not my choice. How *did* I get into this mess?"

It was 1970 when I fell head-over-heels in love. It was a good falling. I had met my soul mate. On our first real date, we went to see *Dr. Zhivago*, but left after twenty minutes, laughing and running breathless from the theater. Not that the movie was bad, but we were anxious to talk. We had missed so much in the years it had taken to find each other.

"We'll have to get married so we can finish a conversation and still get some sleep," Ronnie half-joked.

We spent our first four years together working and playing, relying heavily on the advice of my mother-in-law: "Plan on giving eighty percent and getting twenty."

I was like a butterfly emerging from a cocoon, discovering talents and goodness, previously dormant, becoming the person my husband saw, far better than my own vision.

I let him slay the dragons in my life.

In 1974, we welcomed the first of five daughters, all born in a six-year period. "Let's find some land in the country," my husband suggested. "It's a great place to raise kids. We could have chickens and cows and even horses."

"Just remember, I'm a city girl," I told him. "I'm scared to death of big animals. And most of the small ones, too."

"No problem there. I'll handle the 'wildlife.' You'll love the peace and quiet."

He was right. I also loved the physical labor, especially the process of digging and planting in the newly tilled soil. I was fascinated by the cycle of life that sifted through my fingers in the spring and softly slid through my hands in the fall, finding rest in sterilized jars.

I dug the fence posts that divided my half-acre from the five and a half the animals occupied. Ronnie hoed the irrigation rows and prepared the soil.

We planted fruit trees and grapes at midnight by a full moon, afterwards sharing a quiet moment on the front porch swing, listening to a chorus of frogs and crickets. This was life as it should be.

I learned to milk cows, collect eggs, and churn cream into butter, life-sustaining skills that built my confidence. I taught myself to sew curtains and matching bedspreads, and one year, made five matching Easter dresses for the girls, finishing just in time.

It was that Saturday night, between Good Friday and Easter morning, as I wound yet another strand of wet blonde hair onto a pink sponge curler, that my father called.

"Is your sister still there?" he asked. His voice sounded so strained, I wondered if they'd had a disagreement, but she would have told me.

"No, she's been gone an hour, Dad."

Twenty minutes later when I heard three car doors slam outside, the earlier emotion in my father's voice pierced my heart.

Before opening the door, I knew my husband was dead. The small plane he had been on never reached its destination.

Suddenly, I was sole dragon slayer and ill prepared. I had become dependent on someone else for protection, support, and, yes, even my happiness.

Although I had gained in physical strength, life skills, and self-confidence, I would only feel overwhelming loss for a long time. I was so alone, and so helpless. Not even a flicker of light shone on the horizon.

"How could the world still exist," I asked, "without him in it?"

"'Mom!" Ashley, my oldest preschooler, interrupted my afternoon reminiscing.

"Carrie's crying."

"What, Honey? Oh, I'm sorry. I didn't realize anyone was awake... Quick, help me get the kids in the car. We need to meet the school bus."

"Can we take the wagon?" her eager blue eyes pleaded with mine.

I glanced at the red wagon, lying on its side, the handle bent at an unnatural angle. Rust had overtaken the paint. It had been our favorite mode of transportation to meet Daddy on his way home from work. The memory hit like a physical blow.

"We don't have time," I responded curtly.

It was better than crying and making her feel worse, I reasoned. Besides, there really wasn't time. I still had to outwit the horses before dark.

By then, I had learned to dig furrows myself, and irrigating was a minor task. I had even taken the farmer who shared the head gate with me to small claims court, because he had decided to lock the gate when he didn't want me using it. I was amazed at my own boldness as I stood before the local judge and explained my case.

But I still hadn't learned how to handle the horses.

Neither had I figured out something else, something much more important.

"I don't know how to help the girls with their grief—I don't even know how to cope with my own," I had confided in a neighbor as we made grape jelly.

"How do you explain that Daddy left for a short flight one morning but the plane never made it back, to a child who is barely old enough to understand the concept of time?"

"I think you need to start dating," my neighbor answered. "There're lots of eligible guys where I work who'd love to go out with you. It isn't natural to be alone. I certainly don't plan on staying that way."

"Maybe you're right. I guess it couldn't hurt."

"Certainly no more than being divorced," she was referring to her situation. "I don't know why it couldn't have been my husband instead of yours on that plane. Then we'd all be happy."

Dating was awkward and uncomfortable at first. I was twenty-nine but felt like a kid back in high school. It was fun, though, and a distraction from all my problems. My life had more variety, and more adult conversation, again.

One night, I came in late, dropped into bed, and drifted into a deep sleep. A thud above my head startled me awake. The full moon shining behind my white curtains outlined a huge creature in the windowsill. I shrieked and leapt out of bed, my heart pounding in my ears. The dark form jumped on the bed and yowled as I sprang for the light.

"Mommy, Mommy! It's dus da tat da sitter let in," my three year old explained as I raced down the hallway, swinging a broom and yelling at the frightened stray. I threw open the door, and when the cat gladly shot out, slammed and bolted it.

Gathering my alarmed children in my bed, it seemed hours before my heart slowed down and sleep once again closed my eyes.

Standing at the kitchen sink the next morning, observing the beginnings of spring, I had a flashback. Ronnie and I were on our first camping trip in our "new" second-hand trailer. Everything had gone wrong, from a moldy smell in the mattress to one of the corner jacks falling in the middle of the night!

But like most bad experiences, the telling had become a source of humor. I felt myself smiling. It felt good to smile. At that moment, I knew I was finally healing.

"Ashley," I said later that day, "let's go clean up the wagon so we can pull it to the bus stop." My daughter's face beamed as she raced to get a bucket and rags.

As the wagon creaked down the bumpy lane, I surveyed our home and the acreage that surrounded it. My husband's memories would always be locked in my heart, but it was time to move on.

Rather than sell the house and animals, I said "yes" to remarriage.

Although I have always hated confrontation and fighting, my new spouse seemed to thrive on it.

I had been taught to value hard work and responsibility. In the seven years we were married, my new husband never held a job more than eight months consecutively. I had no desire to own my own business, but let him convince me he could be his own boss, running a convenience store.

It had been an attraction of opposites. A disastrous one until I found the courage to break free. The butterfly that had emerged from my first marriage staggered from the second with tattered wings.

Yet I now had a son, Jackson, who made the union worthwhile if nothing else good had come of it. And I was stronger, having had to take care of myself even while married. I wanted to help other women do the same.

"I hear you ended up with the store," remarked Ian, a psychologist who had invited me to co-lead relationship groups with him.

"By default, more or less," I said as we arranged chairs for a group about to start. "But it does provide some income.

"I'm lucky to have good employees, so I can be home when the kids get off the bus until they go to bed.

"I can also take Jackson to work with me during the day."

"Don't you get scared working late at night by yourself?" Ian asked.

"Not really," I shrugged. "I used to keep a gun with me, but decided I'd probably end up getting shot with it myself.

"Actually, the worst experience I've had was responding to the burglar alarm at three in the morning. When I pulled into the parking lot, three deputies assumed a 'knowing' position with high-powered rifles pointed right at me. Now that was scary!"

"What about all the repairs?" Ian asked. "Don't you miss your ex handling those?"

"I find it's a lot cheaper to hire a repairman than to support a husband," I laughed. "I'm amazed at how skewed my thinking was. I had no idea how damaged my self-esteem was until I got out of that marriage.

"I honestly thought I couldn't survive alone. That seems so silly now."

"Let's see if we can convince this group of that," he said, as our members started arriving.

It was right after my second husband left on my request, after not making yet another deposit at the bank, causing checks I had written to bounce all over the place, that I marched out to the pasture to make sure the animals had water. I yanked open the gate and stomped past the horses, unaware they had stopped their chewing to observe this "stranger."

After checking the trough, noting how well my last fix-it job had held, I noticed the sun setting over the hills, throwing orange and red flames across the sky. On my way back to the gate, I suddenly stopped in front of my former enemies.

They were still staring at me when I reached out to rub the largest one's snout. He flinched a little, but let me get closer. I wrapped my arm around his neck and buried my face in his mane, smelling the sweat and dirt of years unattended.

I began to cry, but not out of sadness. I had finally slain the biggest dragon of them all—something far bigger than a horse—the fear of being alone.

Welcome the Seasons
by Ann E. Byrnes

When speculators purchased the riverside farm, they closed its orchard, which had provided produce to local Eastern Shore residents for decades. Several years later, Susan, a trim woman with a degree in horticulture, purchased the property with an inheritance from her grandfather. Winter succumbed to spring, and the surviving fruit trees, although neglected and overgrown, came alive. Susan joined the rejuvenation—pruning, weeding, fertilizing.

An old mural, entitled WELCOME THE SEASONS, inspired her. Tucked under the north-facing overhang of the beekeeper's shed, the illustration spilled across wooden planks, depicting scenes from the farm—the barn, peach trees in bloom, beehives and berry patches, crop fields, fruit-laden apple trees, children skating on the pond, a sunset. She wondered who had painted it so many years ago.

SPRING

Although she had heard much about Annice Fike, the former owner and a well-respected figure in the community, it was not until May, when Annice returned to the farm for a quart box of early strawberries, that the two women met.

Susan smiled and extended a berry-stained hand to welcome her visitor. Annice noticed that Susan was about the same age she had been when her son married and folks began to call her "Old Mrs. Fike" to distinguish her from her daughter-in-law. "Funny," she mused, "I never gave it a second thought at the time, but I really was too young to be called that."

"I planted many of these trees myself," she told Susan as they walked through the orchard toward the strawberry patch. "They grow, blossom, bear fruit. In time they wear out, and you plant new seedlings. The land moves in its cycles, just as we do. My husband and I came to the end of one cycle. Transplanted ourselves into town."

"You must miss the farm," Susan replied.

"Parts of it I do," Annice answered. "But we have no regrets. The boys weren't interested in taking over. Not enough money in it for the labor,

31

you know. We lived at the mercy of nature and the economy. It was time for us to move on."

When they reached the beekeeping shed, Annice announced, "When I was a young girl, I painted this mural for 4-H. Oil paints were a luxury back then. It took me almost a year to save up the money. Won the grand prize, 1936."

Crows feet whispered around Susan's green eyes as Annice inspected each detail, noting hay bales, wildflowers, livestock, ladders, tools. Reaching, she touched the texture of the surging pink blossoms. "This is me," she said, pointing to a skater on the pond. "Look at the detail on Daddy's tractor, right down to the gauges."

As they walked back to her car, Annice's voice, soft yet strong, echoed her father's. "Daddy used to say I'd made a picture of the Eleventh Commandment: 'Thou shalt consider my seasons.' Whenever one of us needed to sort something out, Daddy would send us out to study my mural. 'There's nothing happening that's not happening in its own season,' he'd say. 'It's up to us to do the welcoming.'"

Annice clasped Susan's forearms. "You've done well by the old place."

Sitting on the back steps, Susan ate a pint of strawberries straight from the hulls, tasting the symphony of the now-petaled land.

SUMMER

Susan's tanned skin was moist with perspiration. She had tied her honey-colored hair back against the breathless heat. Her white cotton tee-shirt and worker's apron were stained with peach drippings, raspberry juice, remnants of wildflower bouquets, soil, and driblets of her own blood.

The sun had already set behind the timothy fields, checkered with freshly-baled hay. She was tending the livestock and closing the barn for the night, so did not see him approaching. In his hand he carried a bag of peaches, just purchased from the stand at the side of the house.

Impulsively, she glanced toward his car to see if his wife had accompanied him. The vehicle was empty, except for his dog.

The man looked at her as he always had, with unspoken indications. "Summertime agrees with you," he pronounced in his southern accent. Unassumingly genteel.

He still had that way of gently touching her arm in greeting so that she was unsure if it was a token of affection, a gentlemanly gesture, or "a way of getting an answer 'yes' without asking any clear question."[2]

Here was the teacher who had, less than ten years ago, introduced her to science—concepts such as "nature loves symmetry" and the restoration of equilibrium in a chemical equation. They had talked of how the behavior of certain stress-relieving chemical reactions was similar, if not identical, to the reactions of organisms. When threatened by disaster, don't living things respond by rallying their defenses, resetting themselves to a healthy balance? And, when disturbed, don't humans counter crisis, change, even infatuation by seeking a new center and shifting to a correct disposition?

Knowing him had changed her. He had upset her equilibrium with a heated, mysterious nature, a chemistry she could never explain. Like a seed that buds but does not blossom, fraught with purpose, but failing at fruition, what had been between them reacted in a fragmentary development, a mutation of nature's systematic tendencies.

As he drove away, his dog panted out the window. Susan stood watching, enfolded in the twilight, long after the taillights disappeared. In the sultry stillness, her mind returned to a place from the past that, like the growth rings of a tree, would always be with her.

AUTUMN

Autumn brought its vague, unsteady sense of coolness and change. Perched on wooden ladders set on frost-covered ground, the migrant workers steadily picked ripened apples. Susan learned of their lives as their voices fell from the branches.

"Carlos left again last night. Looking for work in the city."

"Good riddance if you ask me."

Then a pause. "I'm pregnant again."

A heavy sigh. The slap of a hand against the top of the ladder. "It's beyond me why you let him near you. At least you could use something. You got three kids already."

"Carlos says we should let nature follow its course."

---

[2] Albert Camus

"Carlos says! *Y tu? Que tu dices?* So what are you going to do? Winter'll be here soon."

"If I know Carlos, he'll return by Christmas. He'll have made enough money to last till next spring."

Each day, Susan sold as much fruit as the workers could pick. Each afternoon she paid them, cash counted out into their palms. When one did not show up for work the next day, she wondered why but did not ask. For their unsettled cycles seemed to match the ambiguity of this transient season.

WINTER

Snow covered the land, a patchwork quilted with the remains of one harvest and the tender budding of the next. Pruning equipment stood among the bare branches of the orchard.

School was closed for the Christmas holiday, and the banter of skaters on the pond could be heard from the barnyard. As Susan walked toward the house, Annice drove up the lane for a half-bushel of cold storage apples.

"We always take homemade applesauce to my mother on New Year's Day," she said. "Do you have any apples from those grafted trees down by the horse pasture?"

"In the spring house," Susan pointed.

Once there they discovered an old pair of skates hanging from a rusty hook in the stone wall.

The two women hiked together toward the pond. A crackling campfire punctuated the bitter cold afternoon.

Annice sat on the stump of an oak tree, next to other skaters who were resting. As she laced the timeworn skates onto her small feet, she recounted the events of the violent summer storm that had felled the giant tree, and how the hardwood harvest had warmed the farmhouse kitchen for years afterward. "They still fit," she exclaimed as she wobbled to the edge of the ice.

Susan steadied the old woman for the first few turns around the ice. But once reacquainted with the rhythm of her runners, Annice glided gracefully amid the children, welcoming yet another season with the open arms of her winter dance.

Friends Again
by Dianne Lorang

Ann[3] is a dancer. Although she is one of my oldest friends, I won't know this side of her until we are in our thirties. In fact, she won't know she can dance herself until she is eighteen, married, and has a baby. She is living in Kansas City at the time and decides to take ballet lessons. She catches on fast, studies in New York, and, when she moves back to our hometown in Montana, opens a ballet school. Shortly after that, she founds the Montana Ballet Company.

Ann starts producing *The Nutcracker* every December, offering our little berg a tradition usually only enjoyed by larger cities. She slowly increases the company's shows to four a year, one at the end of a two-week, region-wide workshop in the summer that stars dancers from New York. I know how hard she works as I serve on her board of directors for a while, the last time I live in Montana.

When Ann and I first meet, in junior high school, we are part of a popular group of girls, eight in all. We huddle every morning in the same spot in front of the school, no matter how cold it is. Another girl is our self-appointed leader. Why not, as she is a cheerleader. I'm not even close to being a cheerleader. I am flat-chested and just got glasses. Ann is a lot like me. She comes from a nice family in a nice neighborhood and her father is a professor. Her mother gives Christmas teas.

My mother heads up political committees and I've met several unsuccessful Republican candidates in my home. These would-be important people will soon be replaced by pregnant teenagers whom my mother takes in, I assume, in my self-absorbed way, as a warning to me. Later I realized it was my mother's way of supporting the Pro-Life movement. Anyway, these girls tell me all about sex and boys long before I care. I am a late developer.

Ann jumps ahead of me in that sense. I don't know this until she throws me a surprise birthday party (which I know about since I answered the phone when she called to speak to my mother, and then listened on the extension). I use the bathroom by her and her younger sister's bedrooms. There is a large yellow flowered urn on the counter. I take off the lid and

---

[3] A different Ann, not editor Ann E. Byrnes.

peek in. Ick! A used sanitary napkin. I am the last in our group of friends to cross the threshold into womanhood.

It will be high school before I finally have my first period, at sixteen. I fake it for months, begging out of taking a shower after gym class for a week at a time so everyone thinks I'm normal. In the 1960s, we still wear sanitary belts and very seldom use tampons. Maybe they are too big and bulky for our young bodies. Maybe they are too expensive. Or more likely, they are thought to be harmful, perhaps damaging to our virginal status.

One thing is for sure, we are all virgins, even in high school, or so I think.

But back to junior high, to ninth grade, when our group of eight splits into two groups of four. I don't know why, except Ann has become better friends with the girl next door over the summer, and I become a part of their little group. A new girl is our fourth member—I don't know what happened to the original eighth member, perhaps she moved. That happens often in our college town.

Anyway, it doesn't matter, as we are still part of a group. We still have friends to have slumber parties with, listen to Beatles' albums with, and, believe it or not, walk hand-in-hand through the hallways at school with.

Our little group is singled out by the vice principal who calls us into her office to tell us to befriend a new girl, an ugly girl, a bony girl with buck teeth who doesn't shave her armpits, though, unlike me, she really needs to. It doesn't work. You can't force teenagers to be friends with anyone.

We go to the school dances to meet our boyfriends, the only place we see them outside of school. We go steady with them by wearing their initial rings from Woolworths on chains around our necks. We wear dresses every day, even when it is twenty below zero outside. Mini-skirts have just hit Montana. The "summer of love," 1969, is just around the corner.

It comes after my brother graduates from high school and *doesn't* get drafted and sent to Vietnam. We watch the first moon landing on our black and white television, just like we watched the funerals of Martin Luther King and Bobby Kennedy the year before.

Ann and her best friend have gotten color televisions as they live in a better neighborhood. My parents almost built there, but decided they wanted to be in the country. It would have changed my life. I would have been closer to my friends, closer to the popular kids, not so isolated from the changes in the world. (But then again, I might not have become a writer.)

When we hit high school that fall, something is really different. I am suddenly on my own. Ann is sitting across from me in mass communications class where we have our desks in a big circle. She is wearing beads, a long gypsy-like skirt, and a yellow bandana. She doesn't even look at me. She looks unhappy, even though the boy next to her and she are obviously a couple.

Her locker is close to mine since our last names start with the same two letters. (Lockers, like seats, are assigned alphabetically.) Yet we hardly speak.

But I am a survivor and make friends with two other girls close in the alphabet to me. By the next year, I am bouncing from friendship to friendship, looking for a best friend. It is something I will never really have again.

When I get married at nineteen, I choose a girl I barely knew when we were seniors to be my maid of honor. My second bridesmaid is a girl I've met in college, the girlfriend of one of my fiancé's roommates. The third bridesmaid is my sister who is two years younger.

My mother is a little upset with me because I don't use my three sisters to stand up with me, but my baby sister is only nine years old and my fiancé is only using one of his three brothers as a groomsmen. I already told my two "good" friends from high school, the ones I met at the lockers when Ann ignored me, that I didn't want them to be in my wedding because they'd put a balloon on Jesus' nose when we were decorating my fiancé's house for a party.

They'd laughed and I'd gotten really quiet. Jesus, after all, had been the only one who'd loved me as a child, and now, too, except for my fiancé. Girlfriends are not to be trusted. They always seem to put themselves, or worse, boys first.

The last time I see Ann before I get married is May of our senior year, in her boyfriend's old red panel truck at the drive-in where I work. He, who is "old" himself, twenty-six, comes in to order burgers and shakes and she stays in his truck, eyes staring ahead, not acknowledging me although she knows I am there.

I won't know for ten years or more that she is pregnant and getting married right after graduation. Just like I didn't know she had a dream as a child about ballerinas. The dream was so real, she would tell me, that she'd actually see its dancers on stage when she went to the school auditorium for a symphony. The same auditorium where her ballet company would perform starting in the 1980s. The same auditorium where, in 1972, I played the mother in our high school musical, *Bye Bye Birdie*.

But something happens to that performing part of me when I meet my future husband, about the same time Ann's creative side is awakening in Kansas City. I stop wanting to sing and play the piano, even in church. I give up my dream to be an actress on Broadway. My mother has told me and I believe that "good Christian girls don't go into show business."

I want to be a good girl. I want to be a wife, a mother. I have no reason to finish college, have a career. I have been trained to cook and sew and clean house. I know how to sort laundry, bake bread, and clean nipples of baby bottles. I know how to grocery shop and pick up my siblings from their various activities after school. So I get married, even though I don't have to.

Ann and I meet again in the mid-1980s. It is on Main Street in our hometown in late summer. I am with my oldest daughter who is around ten and Ann is with her daughter, who is a year or so older. Although I've been living here my whole adult life, aside from two years when I was first married, I don't know Ann has a ballet studio above the old Ellen Theater. I immediately sign up my daughter, without asking her if that's what she wants. It must be a way for me to reconnect with Ann.

My daughter's first and only recital is in June the next year. My husband, our three children, and I move to Denver, Colorado, literally, that afternoon.

I see Ann again when we move back three years later. This time, I have changed. My children are all in school and I have returned to college. I am in the process of throwing off my old religion and the "bondage of slavery" it held in my life. I am seeking my true self, what I want out of life.

Ann will be a big part of my transition, for she, too, has started a new life. She has left her husband and has moved into an apartment in town. They were living twenty miles in the country, in an old Dutch farming community, surrounded by his family, just so he could have a barn with a loft for his sculpture studio.

She is now closer to her sister and mother and grandmother and work. Her father died a few years ago. In fact, that is why we embrace when we see each other on the street. She thanks me for the sympathy card I sent her.

I need an old friend like Ann, as it is hard to move back to my hometown. I don't particularly want to be around my family during this semi-rebellious stage in my life. Although they disapproved of my getting married so young, they don't seem to understand why I am going to college now. I am, they think, happily married, and since my husband has a good job, why would I want to be anything but a housewife?

Nor do I want to be around my old church friends, those who haven't moved away or left the church themselves. I'm just one of those girls, as the song says, who wants to "have fun." And fun I have, with Ann. Her boyfriend, who owns the music store on Main Street, is in the rock 'n' roll band that plays at the dance bar on weekends. I go there with Ann to listen to him play, and we dance in front of the giant speakers.

Ann is a free spirit in her short skirt and I feel halfway attractive just being with her. I am thin, like her, but it has been so long since any male was interested in me, other than my husband, that I wouldn't know how to react if one approached me the way they approach Ann. She is a true friend, and a good friend, as she turns them all away to hang out with me.

She ditches me, though, as soon as her boyfriend is on break. That's okay. I can handle a few minutes by myself. I see some people I know from college and visit with them at their table. Sometimes Ann and I stay until closing; she goes out to breakfast with the band and I go home to my children. If my husband is in town, he might meet us and then the four of us go out to breakfast.

Other times Ann and I leave early. We cruise the drag in her black Camaro, like we *didn't* do together in high school, before going back to her place for a cup of herbal tea. We talk for an hour or so about the shackles of marriage, the frustrations of motherhood, and her problem getting her boyfriend to commit, even to just living together.

Once, rather than go back to her place, I tell her about the professor I have a crush on and we drive by his house to see if he's still up. We almost stop and ring the doorbell, like girls would in high school. The plan is to run away, but in my fantasy life, he answers the door, invites me in, and Ann disappears, the way I disappear when her boyfriend decides to come over to her place to spend the night.

Just for a change of pace one night, we go out to the Karaoke bar and I get up and sing "These Boots are Made for Walking," from the Nancy Sinatra record I still own. Men buy me drinks to keep me singing, and although I don't drink them, I oblige until I run out of songs.

Dianne Lorang

It is fun to perform again. I try out for a musical at college but am not right for the part. A sexy young thing gets it, but at least I try. And I take keyboard lessons to learn to play the piano by ear rather than just by reading music. Ann is learning the electric guitar and we are going to form a band. Our plan is to play at our twentieth high school reunion. I'm glad we don't get our act together in the end. "What a dead crowd this is," we say to each other. "How terribly 'unfun' these old people are."

Ann has just broken up with her boyfriend, or he has broken up with her. It won't be the last time. I move back to Denver the next summer with my husband and two youngest children. My oldest daughter has graduated from high school and is going to college in the East. Ann has a rough winter, waking up one morning with Bell's Palsy. Half of her face is paralyzed. She thinks it could be from the chemicals used in the remodeling of her new dance studio. Her condition more or less heals by spring, but her big smile will always be down a little on one side.

She and her boyfriend get back together and even live together for a while, but it doesn't last. He cheats on her with a younger woman, who just happens to look like Ann. Eventually, he will marry his new girlfriend and buy my grandmother's house from my parents, who live there for a few years after her death.

Although Ann is past the prime age for a ballerina, she is still beautiful and attractive and able to perform along with her students and the professional dancers she brings to town to add to the culture of Montana.

To me, she is like Anne Bancroft in the movie, *The Turning Point*. I am like her friend, Shirley MacLaine, who gave up so many possibilities to raise a family. Yet we have more in common now than when we first met in junior high. We are both strong women who have learned to be happy, independent of the men in our lives. We have both gone after our dreams, and lived them, and continue to find our way in the world.

Ann and I don't e-mail, we don't write, we don't call each other on the phone. But whenever I'm in Montana, I get in touch and we go to breakfast or lunch or sometimes dinner. We have the best time catching up on each other's lives, talking mostly about work or bragging about our grown children.

As we live out the second half of our forties, we are still those young girls with hope in their eyes who were part of a group of friends in junior high school. Only now we know *why* we are friends.

Daddy's Good Girl
by Chandra K. Clarke

She felt chewed, mauled, ground up. Spit out. It was as though the chewing had left her with gaping holes, the wind whistling through her. God, how it hurt. She looked at the headstone in front of her. It was gray, like the sky. It was wet, like the ground. And cold, hard, bleak. It said: *James Rahl 1964-1996.*

She lay down beside the grave, looking up. The clouds above were one large faceless mass; the rain left them endlessly in a continuous drizzle. It pattered on the grass, on her coat, on her hands. She blinked rapidly in the onslaught.

She wondered what they would say, what they would think, when they found her body. How long would it take? She imagined how they would see her: the too-thin arms, the too-thin legs, the mass of tangled brown hair, and the pale skin, spotted with freckles. A plain face. A plain body. Shapeless clothes: an old pair of jogging pants, battered shoes, a frayed tee-shirt. A thin gold necklace.

She reached up and pulled it taut. It cut into the back of her neck, making a bright red line against the white flesh. It quivered and twisted with the force, biting deeper and deeper...

"Don't do that," her father had told her. "Don't do that or you'll break it. Be my good girl."

She had stopped of course. She was Daddy's good girl.

They lived in a cute two-bedroom bungalow on Main Street, painted blue with a nice front garden. The flowers smelled fresh and sweet. Her father cut the grass and her mother did the dishes. They had a cat named Powderpaw. They had nice neighbors with a little girl who would come over to play.

She went to the quiet little elementary school across the street and got good grades because her mother told her she should. Her father told her to stay off the dangerous playground equipment, so she did. She played with Barbies and toy tea sets because that's what she got on her birthdays.

They all went to church on Sundays and her father would say, "Have you met my daughter?"

The rain turned cold. It traced icy fingers along her body, sucked at her bones, chilled her flesh. She could feel herself sinking deeper into the soft, cool, brown mud. She pulled the necklace again, harder and harder, until it snapped. It slithered away from her fingers and buried itself in the murk.

It had been a year since James had died. Where had the time gone? A year of drifting and floating, sleeping late, and watching the small TV until the wee hours of the morning. She remembered the rain and snow that had come and gone. There were people outside, laughing and talking. People on TV having fun, being together. She couldn't remember sunshine.

Her first day of high school had been bright and sunny, the light streaming in through the windows, dancing along the corridors. Her mother had gone to this high school. Some of the older teachers greeted her as Judi's girl.

So this was what it was like to almost be an adult! The school heaved and pulsed with action and adventure. She had responsibilities, such homework as she'd never seen, places to go, and a schedule to keep. There were so many people. She made new friends, nice girls from all over the county with fresh faces and good clothes. They played sports and giggled in the hallways.

The library had so many books! Sweet romances, stories of foreign lands and exotic peoples who lived differently. How she longed to visit those countries and meet them. There were so many things she could be! There were so many possibilities, she wanted to try them all. She was a young woman. She began to think, and to see…

She closed her eyes against the pounding rain. The last year had been cloudy, a blur of time and distance. She had felt surrounded by fog, numb and unanchored. Everything was the same. Color, texture, smell, taste, sound. Only one thing had penetrated her senses, one word, with the power to sear through the haze.

"Alone."

The word ripped at her, tore at her, like a big, black, slavering dog with blood in its eyes.

"Alone."

God, how it hurt.

Her father had said "yes," she could go to the dance. "My daughter's first night out," he had said.

The dance was in the school auditorium. It was her second year of high school, and the auditorium was decorated in fall colors: burnt oranges, muted reds, yellows, and soft browns. It was beautiful and magical. The air outside smelled clean and crisp, with a hint of snow. "I promise," it whispered.

She was just fifteen.

One of her friends picked her up in a car—how grown up! They laughed all the way to the school. The lights inside were turned way down, and the music turned way up. All the girls danced in the center of the auditorium, while the guys watched from the sides with shy, sullen eyes.

When the music suddenly slowed, the girls began to scatter, desperate, hopeful, trying to ignore the slow dance pouring out of the speakers. Then the guys began to move, one by one. The bravest among them circled the girls stealthily, hunting for their choices and darting in to pull the girls away, separating them from the group.

Someone grabbed her hand. "What's your name?" he asked.

"Paula," she said.

"I'm James. Let's dance."

So they did. He smelled nice, and felt strong, and held her very close.

Without opening her eyes, she flexed her left hand and felt the weight there. The cold water seeped underneath, making it easy to slip the ring off. James' high school ring.

She ran her fingers over the stone in the ring, its thick shoulders, its thin band. The rain washed it, running over the gold and silver accents. She knew without looking that the writing said *Westmount Collegiate*, that the little symbol was a graduation cap, and that the gem was red.

Red like the eyes of a dog.

"Alone," the dog growled. "You are alone."

They did things. He'd meet her at the corner and drive her to school. They'd find a quiet spot on the front lawn to eat their lunch. He'd follow her when she was walking with her friends and try to catch her attention. They left notes in each other's lockers. He wrote her name on his arm in big black marker strokes.

Her friends rolled their eyes every time he came around; when he left they'd pounce on her and ask for details. The teachers smiled benignly at them as they walked through the halls, hand in hand.

The ring had always been too large of course. It was meant for a man's right hand, not a woman's left. It was a wonder she hadn't lost it. Perhaps it was because she'd always kept her hands in tight fists.

"What do you mean you're pregnant?" Daddy had yelled. So many people had seen it coming, the storybook with the tragic ending, why hadn't she? "What do you mean you're pregnant?" he yelled again.

How could she tell him that James had said it was okay, that it would be fun, except that it wasn't because he went too fast? How could she tell him that James had been kind and sweet and nice, and called her by name? She hadn't meant for it to happen. She hadn't told James yet.

"Do you realize what you've done to me?" Daddy yelled. "I have a pregnant daughter. I'm ruined."

So ruined was he that he threw her out.

She never knew what her mother had said. She went to James and told him. He sat there quietly, for what seemed like hours. Then he grabbed her by the hand and pulled her towards the door.

"Where are we going?" she asked.

"We're gonna make you Mrs. James Rahl," he replied.

She let the ring drop, heard the gentle splash as it disappeared into the growing puddles around her. Her clothes were soaked. Every inch of her body was wet. Would they find her jewelry when they found her body? Would they know who she was?

"Who am I?" She wondered.

The ceremony was brief and brutal—a few minutes with the justice of the peace in a bustling downtown office. A few words, a signature, and it was over. The storybook continued, its predictable pages spread out before them.

James left her at his parents' house and went away for a while. He came back with a black eye and all her clothes. Her friends, good girls all, quit speaking to her. She quit school. James got a job at a grocery store.

Then there were fights with his parents, and they had to move out. They took the little apartment over the store. At least it was clean.

James invited his friends from school and his friends from work over every Friday night. She served them food and beer, and if there was anyone new, James would say, "This is my wife."

Time passed and the baby came, after a long, hard labor. He was James all over again—black eyes, black hair, and strong. He smelled nice, too. They called him Jimmy.

The rain stopped. The sudden silence was deafening. Nothing moved; there was no breeze. Nothing dripped. The dog hovered.

Jimmy grew, as children do. He went to school, got in trouble with the teachers, and made lousy marks in class. There was no money; she wasn't allowed to work. James started drinking more. A few beers on Friday night turned into a few beers every night, until the first order of business after work was to get drunk.

She spent her time cleaning, feeding Jimmy, and going for walks. Very long walks, under washed-out skies. Jimmy called her Mom, when he wanted something.

When Jimmy was old enough, James sent him to a different high school on the other side of town. He didn't give a reason. She had to drive him there every morning and home again every night. Jimmy hated it. He cut classes, chased girls, stayed out late at night. He smashed the windows of the grocery store. The cops brought him home.

Then one night Jimmy went out and didn't return. James left the house and came back with a broken nose. "He's not coming home," he said and got drunk again.

Jimmy was just fifteen.

A year later, James lost his job at the grocery store, went out for a long drive with a tall bottle, and wrapped the car around a telephone pole. She wore her black jogging pants and tee-shirt to the funeral, covering them up with her best coat. All his friends came and wept over his coffin. Said they'd be around if she needed them. None of them called again. Not once, in a year.

She shivered. She opened her eyes and saw that the skies were broken now, no longer an endless gray blanket. The wind picked up a little, blowing at the trees, puffing gently at the clouds above.

She saw them, really looked at them, for the first time. She remembered watching the clouds as a girl, naming each one she saw. They were all different. Some were like animals, others like people. Most were just clouds, unique in shape and form. A few of them clumped together; others strayed away from the group.

"Alone."

The word rushed her, came out of nowhere to attack. It hurt, yes, it hurt.

But somehow the hurt felt...different.

"Alone."

She tasted the word, felt it between her teeth, rolled it on her tongue.

"Alone. On my own.

"I am on my own."

She shifted uncomfortably in the mud. She felt so heavy, so solid against the mush.

"I am thirty-two."

The realization struck her. "I was with him for longer than I was without him. And I wasn't even me yet when I met him.

"Who am I?"

She reached into her pocket and pulled out a five-dollar bill and a driver's license. "They would have known had they found my body," she thought. "They would have known who I was."

Her picture stared back at her. It was a bad picture, but the eyes still looked clear. The hair needed combing, but it was still free of gray.

The name underneath said *Paula Damalis Rahl*.

Paula lifted her arm from the sucking, grasping mud, and drew her thumbnail across the last name. She did it again. And again and again until the paper frayed and scraped away.

The name underneath now read *Paula Damalis*.

"Gracious dear, are you all right?" An old woman peered down at her with a worried expression on her face. "Are you all right?"

Paula sat up. Water fell from her hair and made her shirt stick to her back.

"Who are you?" she asked.

"Margaret," the woman replied. "I live in the city. Every once in a while I come out here to visit my son."

Paula looked around. "Your son is here?"

Margaret nodded and pointed to a distant headstone. "Yes. Over there. The tall stone with the cross on top. He's beside his father. He died four years ago in a car accident. Lord, but I miss him."

Paula stared. She cleared her throat awkwardly and wiped her eyes. "His father? Can I…can I ask how?"

The other woman looked surprised. "My husband, you mean? Why, killed in the war of course. Silly man went off to fight and left me with three children and a farm to look after. Which is why I live in the city now," she winked, and then sighed fondly. "But he did look sweet in a uniform."

"In the war?" Paula said. "Which war?"

"Gracious girl, what a silly question. The Second World War of course. Got the telegram in the winter of '43, although God knows how long he'd been gone by that time. The mail boys tried hard, but it couldn't have been easy getting news back from the front."

"The winter of '43." Paula heard the phrase over and over again. "The winter of '43." More than fifty years ago.

"Did you remarry?" she had to ask.

Margaret shook her head. "Heavens no. By the time I got all my kids out the door I wasn't the least interested in all that silly courting and dating stuff. I traveled. I've been to Japan you know," she said proudly.

"More than fifty years ago," Paula thought. "She has been without him for longer than I've been alive."

"Listen dear, you never did answer me. Are you all right? You're covered in mud. Do you need any help?"

Paula thought for a minute. "No thank you. I slipped, but I'm fine now." She stood up.

The old woman smiled. "Good for you, dear."

"I'm sorry about your husband and son."

Margaret nodded. "I'll tell them you said so."

Paula smiled hesitantly. She walked away, wet, cold, her stride a bit uncertain but steady, having passed through the gray and beyond.

Abagail
by Dora Marjorie

I tapped on the open door of her room at the rest home. Abagail Abercrombie called from her bed. Entering, I extended my hand to a Katherine Hepburn look-a-like, thin, freckled, her manner and voice belying her ninety-six years. Her hair, snow white, drawn back into a slightly disheveled bun, nestled in the nape of her neck.

In answer to her questioning look, I explained that I had bought her table silver at the recent homestead auction and thought she would appreciate meeting me.

"My silver," she whispered. "I polished it regularly. It meant so much to me. A wedding present from my husband's parents, you know. I'm so delighted it will stay in New Zealand."

A fluttering hand motioned me to an armchair.

"I'd no idea of the life ahead when I married Richard in 1914," she began as though talking to a close friend. "We were only seventeen. Imagine, my dear, *only* seventeen! A case of love at first sight, for neither knew of the other until we met at a woolshed dance.

"Imagine me a partner in a *Romeo and Juliet* affair, a young country lass swept off her feet by a strong and reliable Richard who proved, very quickly, to be the perfect lover!" Her eyes sparkled and flashed in my direction.

"The wedding was a spectacular affair, one of those country weddings where everyone turns up to be both helper and guest. Of course we were photographed as a bridal couple in the usual before-The-Great-War pose: bride standing, groom seated." Her hand gestured toward the dressing table where a silver frame surrounded a brown, sepia photograph.

"I couldn't stop looking at Richard's hands," she said. "For one so young, they were huge, manly things used to hard, farm labour[4]. They electrified me.

"My dress, as you can see, a lovely simple, calf-length frock. Cream satin. Silly me," she said, wiping away a little moisture from her eyes.

"The first months of marriage were hectic as we renovated a shepherd's cottage and toiled on the estate," she continued as her

---

[4] Spelling in this story is in New Zealand English.

49

outstretched hand waved in the direction of the farm many miles inland. "Oh, how we loved!

"I can still feel the excitement of our love and the work we did on that cottage because of that love. From a shack, our love-nest rose like a Phoenix from the ashes. We were intoxicated with the fervour of love."

She paused and looked out the window. Before returning to her tale, she asked me to assist her from her bed and into her armchair.

"When Richard turned eighteen, the Front called, for the sense of Empire was strong, and fighting the Germans the noble thing to do."

Telling me this, Abagail sat bolt upright as if to salute Richard, the British Empire, and all things patriotic. I could almost see her memory of that emotionally charged moment.

"Immediately uniformed, Richard sailed for France in 1915."

"I can imagine how you missed him," I commented.

"How I missed him! However, I'd told him I'd keep the home fires burning. It wasn't easy with his mother so sickly, and the property very short of shepherds. I battled on, often riding into the highest hills to help muster.

"I'm proud of that. I'd just turned eighteen when he left. That's very young to shoulder such responsibility. I think the most difficult part was lambing, for I'd no experience in caring for ewes in difficulty.

"The scatter-brained men the war forced me to employ didn't know either. But I soon learned. It's amazing what you can do when necessity calls.

"Mercifully, after three years of doing his duty, Richard returned, none the worse for wear. But his father had died about two years before and the shock had hastened his delicate mother's end.

"With my absent husband and I owning the property, I had lawyers to deal with and endless business affairs to sort out, as well as organising the day to day running of a large farm with very little able help. Such a responsibility.

"Richard's eventual return filled me with elation. More hard work, of course, but now we did it together. One of the biggest tasks was restoring the homestead and moving into the historic *kauri* building."

Abagail leaned back in her chair as her eyes took on a faraway look. I could see she was back there selecting colors and rearranging furniture.

"Frequently we would take a picnic tea to the river and bathe, letting the chilly waters of the mountain stream and the warm sun caress our naked bodies," Abagail said with a knowing wink in my direction. "At other times we would walk for miles over our pasture land, hand in hand, each silently enjoying the close company of the other.

"Our favourite time was spring when clusters of daffodils, wild and abandoned, and frolicking lambs seemed to symbolise the vibrancy of our love. On bitter, winter evenings we cuddled by the open fire."

"And children?" I asked.

"There were none," she said. "One of us must have been infertile. A child would have been a comfort in my old age, I suppose, but I've no regrets. The work on the farm in those first years demanded long hours of intense labour.

"A family seemed the last consideration. I worked side by side with Richard. No skirt affair I can assure you for I found trousers that fitted, and plunged my feet into sturdy boots."

I nodded in agreement.

"As the years went by, as they do in routine and ritual, I did less and less on the property, settling into life as a pastoralist's wife-worker. Secretly, I missed the hard work. I never let on. Richard seemed determined I would be the 'lady of the manor,' as he termed it.

"We celebrated Christmas in style, throwing large parties, but enjoyed birthdays and wedding anniversaries alone. We always had a special, nonsensical something for the other. Nothing expensive, mind you, just a little something to make us laugh.

"One year Richard gave me a doll's gardening set. He said it would be useful for digging in the garden! That year, as if planned, I had found a lovely toy tractor in a mail order catalogue and sent for it. Thrilled, Richard insisted it sit on his chest of drawers in the bedroom. It looked ridiculous, but served as a reminder of the hard day's toil."

"About five years after The Great War, we were exhausted and took a trip to Europe. In Provencal, after he showed me the scarred, French countryside where he'd fought, Richard bought me a beautiful, antique silver belt." Standing, Abagail opened a drawer and took out the most exquisite, hand-crafted, silver-lace belt.

"It's absolutely magnificent!" I whispered.

"It is, isn't it! And I'm going to wear it to my grave clasped over the cream satin of my wedding dress, just as Richard's arms used to be clasped around me," she said as she lightly clapped her hands together and smiled.

Deeply moved, I waited in silence for her to return to her story.

"I'm still amazed at how strange—no, how *cruel*—life can be. One fateful day, my birthday, one of the men came for me. Richard, thrown from his horse, had collided headlong with a huge boulder. The poor darling died instantly."

"How terrible!"

"Terrible indeed." She stopped just for a second as if saying a silent prayer.

"While I've constantly craved the touch of his vanished hand and the sound of his stilled voice, I had to get along with maintaining the property. I'd a life to live and work to do. Sheep don't look after themselves.

"Continually, I had the problem of hiring men, for our isolation drove many away soon after they arrived. Some drank too much and turned up late for work. Married men with a family were reluctant to come as the only school meant a long bus ride for the children, or correspondence school.

"I lost count of the number of men who came and went, including so-called farm managers. Many, thinking a woman couldn't run things, were extremely rude. Some made demands for extras over and above the agreed wage, trying to beat me down with threats of no work unless I agreed to free meat or a contribution toward their electric power.

"I told them, pointedly, that with our isolation, they were lucky to have power at all. Besides, I cooked generous meals for the single men so I didn't see the need to supply free meat, and I told them so.

"The greatest problem, I think, concerned planning. It helped when the phone arrived, but the service wasn't always reliable. I lived a lonely life, but a healthy and busy one as the only woman about the place for the majority of the time."

"If I may ask, what about money?" I wondered.

"I was financially secure, but wool and lamb prices went up and down with such monotony I never knew just what my income would be from year to year. That's all right if there are no wages to pay, thousands of acres of pasture to maintain, fences to repair, and the rest of it.

"I'm not complaining, for I settled into a routine motivated by grief and the need to survive. I used to say to myself when things got me down, 'Sell, Abagail, old girl, sell.' But I couldn't sell regardless of the problems. I loved that place. I loved the silence and the cold winters and the glorious summers and the hills and the valleys and the hard work. I loved the memory of those golden days with Richard, my dear, dear Richard.

"Some of the shepherds looked at me with longing eyes and one or two hinted at a relationship outside the sort for which they were hired. I soon put their thoughts to rest!" she said with a grin and a nod of her head. "My love for Richard is like the silver you purchased and the silver belt he gave me—durable, everlasting, precious. His death didn't stop that love. I would never need another.

"Instead, I stayed and created a memorial of sorts to his memory. I was determined to remain true to the promise I made when Richard had left for the Front: Should anything happen to him, I'd stay on the property until too old to cope. Prophetic words.

"Fortunately there were, among the rogues and the I-don't-know-anything-about-*that*-types, good men and true men who came and stayed to muster, shear, lamb, and maintain the buildings, cultivate the pastures and the crops, and drench the flock and the rest of it.

"However," she added as she sat straighter and assumed a firm tone of voice, "I ran the business, I hired the men, I attended to the accounts, I cooked the meals for the single men and the shearing gangs, I did the ordering, and I cared for the garden. And, my dear, I'm proud of it!"

Amazed at her tale, but puzzled by the lack of any specific date as to Richard's death, I asked just when her husband had died

Silently, she turned her head slowly away from me toward the window. "Oh," she whispered slowly after a long pause, her voice trembling ever so slightly, "my darling went to his rest sixty-four years ago."

Not as a Tourist
by Ellen Kurtz

Israel, November, 1989. At last, after five hours on a bus, I was close to my destination. The ever-changing colors on the stark, stony mountains were unlike any desert landscapes I had seen in pictures.

Passing through the heart of residential Eilat, the bus moved upward beyond the city limits, until it reached its final destination, Army Base No. 80, high on a rocky hill. It was here that my services were required, where for three weeks I would live with a group composed of strangers. I, at age fifty-five, after spending the first part of my life as a city girl and the rest as a suburban wife and mother, was going to don an army uniform, live in a barracks, and work with soldiers.

Just eighteen months ago, back home in New Jersey, I would never have imagined myself here, surrounded by tanks, trucks, and rifles. Neither would I have dreamt that I could look forward to such an existence...

May, 1988. My favorite time of year. I looked up from the menu as I heard my husband greet the restaurant manager, who knew him by name. Ray was a big man, who stood about a head taller than my five feet, two inches. His dark complexion, strong features, and cheerful face punctuated by a bushy mustache made him stand out among the restaurant's clientele.

"I have a good feeling about this new project," he told me as he sat down, brown eyes sparkling with enthusiasm. "Just wait and see!" He set down a pile of letters he'd brought from the office, part of a marketing campaign we'd worked on that day. His spirit, his sudden spurt of energy, seemed to exude the reawakening of nature around us.

"You know," he said, "after the stock market crash in October, I thought we'd be out of business. But now the rest of 1988 will be great!"

Over won-ton soup, spring rolls, and lemon chicken, we devised the next day's strategy, chatted about our three grown children, and dreamed about a vacation to Israel. We then said our good-byes before separating, he to go to his regular Tuesday evening tennis game, and I to a lecture.

That was the last time I saw him alive. I was preparing for bed when a telephone call told me he'd collapsed on the court. By the time I reached the hospital, he was dead.

Ray, at age fifty-six, had certainly been old enough to be active in civic affairs, to be respected in our community, to head his own investment management business. But—to *die*?

"Cardiac arrest," they told me. "Feels like being hit in the chest with a wrecking ball. It's hard, but very fast."

The doctor ended with a cliché, one meant to comfort me: "He probably didn't know what hit him."

Even in my shock, I knew precisely what had hit *me*. We'd married not long after the Korean War while I was a senior in college and Ray an ensign in the Coast Guard. Though we hadn't met until a campus dance two years before, we'd lived only five blocks from each other and attended the same high school.

As a corporate wife, I had enjoyed entertaining my husband's colleagues and their spouses, and loved accompanying Ray on business trips. Our income was fine for our needs; I always worked part-time because I enjoyed it.

Five years before, I had helped Ray start his business of managing stock investments for pension funds. I knew the company would not survive without him. For all practical purposes, most of my world had just been torn apart.

"You can manage, Ellen," our accountant encouraged me. "Close the business in an orderly fashion. You know I'll help."

It was a relief to know I'd be able to manage financially, and even live comfortably, though without Ray.

Fifty-something is an awkward, in-between age for a widow. Many of your contemporaries are still paired, and you know very few widows in your stage of life.

"For months now I've been picking my way carefully through a new world," I told my sister, who called frequently from her home 350 miles away. "I know I have to gradually reinvent my life as an independent woman, but how?"

It was good to have somebody to talk to, but no matter how supportive my sibling, parents, children, and friends and neighbors tried to be, I was basically on my own, giving myself my own pep talks by day, alone in the emptiness of a big house at night.

I joined a support group for widows. We talked and cried about our losses, our families, our goals. Most of the other women were in their sixties with grandchildren.

"My children are all single and building their own lives," I told them. All three, I hoped, were adjusting to the loss of their father.

"So will you," my newfound friends assured me. Sometimes we'd go out for dinner or even for weekends away.

I started taking temporary writing assignments again, and returned to some of my other interests as well. One day, I startled myself by humming along with a song on the car radio. Not long after that, I found myself laughing, rarely at first, but then more often.

Then I received an intriguing piece of mail from American Veterans of Israel. This was an organization Ray and I both had long felt close to, for his late first cousin, also named Ray Kurtz, had been one of the founders of the Israeli Air Force in 1948. The newsletter said that people were needed to serve for three weeks with a program called Volunteers for Israel. Impulsively, and quite uncharacteristically, I called the organization's New York office for more information.

"You'll be working wherever you're needed," they instructed me. "Bring your own bed linens, towels, and personal supplies. We'll give you housing, food, a uniform, and work boots. You'll live on a military base for about three weeks, with some time off to tour around the country. All you pay for is the cost of your roundtrip ticket."

The Volunteers for Israel program, I learned, began in 1982 in response to a plea for assistance in harvesting crops because soldiers were fighting in Lebanon. Groups were regularly dispatched from South Africa, several European countries, the United States, and Canada to free Israeli troops for training and other military activities.

In exchange, the volunteers would receive several days of organized sightseeing. Airline tickets were good for 180 days, and free stopovers in Europe could be arranged at the end of the program. It didn't take long for me to sign on.

While awaiting the date of my flight, I sent queries to several publications and was rewarded with two writing assignments. Not only would I participate in the daily life of the military base where I was going to work, but I'd also be recording my experiences so others might benefit from them, maybe even participate in the same program in the future.

I flew out of JFK, and away from the reality of a life I wasn't really comfortable with yet anyway, in an El-Al jet with some 250 other American volunteers. Arriving at Israel's Ben Gurion Airport, we were dazzled almost simultaneously by bright sunshine, smiling children eager to present us with flowers and cold drinks, and my college-age niece, Lisa, who had taken a break from a season of European travel to join me in my adventure.

"You're on Bus 17," Lisa and I were told. "It leaves in a few minutes for Eilat."

On the bus was a single woman named Ruth, from Long Island, and Nettie, a few years older than Lisa. Most of the men were in their seventies, including a retired librarian from Boston who had served on the famous immigrant ship, Exodus 1947. He had been wounded in a battle with the British, whose forces controlled what was then Palestine when the ship was turned away from shore.

Two of the women in our group were married and had come with their husbands, even though they knew they'd be staying separately. The six of us women lived in one barracks room smaller than my own lonely bedroom at home, while on the other side of the wall was a similar room for half of the fifteen men in our group. The other men lived in a small cabin not much different next door.

Beyond that building was the shack housing the women's toilet and shower facilities. The male volunteers shared a bathroom just across the road with male soldiers. Female soldiers had their own accommodations nearby, not much different from ours.

The dining hall was located at the foot of a steep road, which wound up through the base. Sunday through Friday morning, we volunteers ate with the soldiers, passing platters of fried eggs, bread, cheese, yogurt, halvah, fruit, and pitchers of sweetened hot tea and coffee. The midday meal generally provided meat, usually chicken or turkey, and salads, as well as rice or potatoes.

Later, Lisa and I would calculate that we worked a total of ten or eleven days, from eight to five. Mostly we cleaned, polished, and packed the machinery, supplies, and medical equipment stored at the base in case of emergency. We were close to the Red Sea, but rather than sand that had to be cleaned away from everything in sight, it was tan-gray dust.

Most visitors to Israel's southernmost point go there for its warm dry climate, sunny beaches, and the delightfully clear waters of the Red Sea. We came to work, but had our evenings free to spend as we chose. We'd sit at the outdoor tables in town, indulging in ice cream or whipped cream covered cakes, watching the people pass by. Americans seemed to be in the minority compared to the many well-dressed Europeans.

I spent one Sabbath north of Tel Aviv at a *moshav*, where residents own their own homes and some acreage but share equipment and various services.

"We have a good life," my young hostess told me. I could see that her home was as well appointed as any I'd seen back home. Her three young children were just as friendly and hospitable as their parents.

"But I worry, for my husband," she confided. "Next month he goes for his annual reserve duty. He'll be away for thirty days. I'll miss him, and I'll worry even more."

A couple in Haifa, who had lived in the country all their lives, told me of their experiences during Israel's earlier wars. Their four children had all served in the army, too.

"I'm only glad I'm getting old," one woman confessed, unbidden. "I don't want to live long enough to see my grandchildren go to war."

And, of course, they all sympathized with me on my loss.

The soldiers I worked with had more tales to tell, of immigration from poverty-stricken countries, of assimilation into Israeli society, and of long hazardous-duty assignments away from their loved ones.

There were holy sites to see, where Lisa and I and the other volunteers walked in the sandaled footsteps of Biblical heroes. We visited places where both ancient battles and recent conflicts had been fought, and marveled that, despite both age-old and modern strife, this was still an incredibly beautiful country where the most common word spoken was the one that means peace, *shalom*. We hated to leave.

Lisa and I landed at JFK on a cold, windy fall evening typical of late November. We arrived home tired, but were revived by a lively greeting from my parents.

My house was brightly lit, warm, spacious, and comfortable. I walked from room to room, reacquainting myself with a familiar painting here, a favorite chair there, and the bathrooms, clean and blessedly private. My bedroom's aura of calmness overwhelmed me, bringing tears, happy tears, to my eyes. Everything looked so different to me now, and better.

Could it have been because I was different? Better? Had my time in another world changed my perspective, helped in my healing?

Two days later, on Thanksgiving, we awoke to a dusting of snow, a serene covering light enough to provide atmosphere but no hazard to driving.

Ellen Kurtz

We celebrated the holiday at my son's house. My daughter, my parents, Lisa, and I. We called Florida to talk to my other son, and later spoke with Lisa's parents and her sister. The photos we took that day show us as a festive family unit, celebrating our reunion after a long separation.

And the best picture of all shows me with a broad smile as I raise my glass in a Thanksgiving toast where I am saying, with great enthusiasm, "To life!"

Visions
by Dianne Lorang

I'm a college student in my mid-thirties, for the fifth time. Every time I try to go back, my husband gets transferred. But this time I'm going to finish. I'm majoring in Philosophy so most of my previous credits will count. I'm also taking English Writing as my minor. I have just left my poetry writing class in old Roberts Hall at Montana State University. Before the long drive home on an ice-covered highway, I stop in the bathroom. I hear a voice from the next stall: "So what childhood experience are you going to write about?"

It is Becky. We are forever friends after that. I would have never spoken to her first, though, except in class, or maybe just to say "hi" when passing her on campus. I am basically introverted, more like unsure of myself, and Becky and I live very different lives. I have three children, one in junior high in town and two in elementary school in the country— my son's fourth-grade class is actually in a little red schoolhouse. I know he'll be president one day, or at least important.

I have a husband who has a good job and we live on some acreage in a cedar-sided house with a covered front porch and a newly finished basement, so my oldest daughter has her own bedroom and bathroom and phone. We have two woodstoves, one upstairs and one in the basement, a double-car garage with openers, and two new vehicles. Mine is a GMC Safari van. It seats eight and will go 500 miles on a tank. We got it when we lived in Colorado, for the long drives home to Montana. The children would recline in their bucket seats and tune in to their own tapes on their own Walkmans.

Becky lives in a mobile home by the airport ten miles on the other side of town, with her boyfriend. He is also a college student and they both work for minimum wage to supplement their student loans. Like me, Becky is a non-traditional student, but she's also a non-traditional person. I like that about her. She always wears skirts and beaded earrings that complement her long, reddish hair. She cares about her appearance.

Although Becky is not quite thirty years old, she has packed a lot into her three decades. She was married for a short time to an alcoholic and drug addict who beat her and ended up in a wheelchair after falling down the stairs one night. Even while in a wheelchair, he pushed her down the

Dianne Lorang

stairs and her back has hurt ever since. She was smart to leave him but is presently fighting off his creditors since he can't pay the bills he rang up when they were man and wife. It's a while before I find out Becky dropped out of high school and got her GED so she could go to college.

I've lived in this conservative college town for most of my life, since my parents divorced in the early 1960s. My dad, the one who raised me and eventually adopted me, is a doctor at the Student Health Center here on campus. That's where he and my mom met when she was a non-traditional student. His parents are cornerstones of the community. My grandmother's[5] family home was where the town's daily newspaper building stands today. She still teaches piano lessons, but I haven't followed my brother by sending my children to her. It was hard on me trying to play good enough for Grandma.

My grandfather was a dean at the college until he retired in 1966. A building was named for him. He died soon after its ribbon-cutting dedication. I was there for all the pomp and circumstance with two of my children. The third hadn't been born yet. I would barely be pregnant with her when we buried Grandpa on a very cold Christmas Eve.

Although I was raised in "high society," partaking in the social gatherings of professors and their wives, going to the local symphony, and bobbing for apples hung on strings (rather than in an unsanitary tub of water) at Halloween parties at doctors' houses, I married a man whose roots were more like my real ones, before my mom remarried. His father was an electrician and his mother an office manager. My mother was a "lady of leisure," even though she worked very hard around the house because she'd learned to from her mother.

Becky grew up in rural Montana. Her father died when she was eleven and she wrote an intense story about his funeral, how she had peed her panties, for another writing class we took together. Her mother would remarry but Becky, like me, had felt abandoned by her father, and been looking for a replacement ever since.

She spent her teen years in turmoil, living on the edge of excitement, not just riding on the back of motorcycles but learning to ride one herself. She would be so excited for me when my husband, in his late forties, would start buying motorcycles and go to Sturgis, South Dakota, for the

[5] A different grandmother, now deceased, than mentioned before by editor Dianne Lorang.

big rally there. She would never know about his Harley Davidson, though, that he finally moved up to the "baddest" bike of them all.

But the last time I would talk to her, I'd show her my youngest daughter's tattoo, a butterfly. She got it on her eighteenth birthday, when children don't need parental consent. I wasn't upset. How could I be when one of my best friends had several tattoos? Becky's last tattoo was the result of a dream—two blue horses all over her back and shoulder, manes blowing in the wind.

She had lots of dreams and visions, even visits from the dead. Her grandmother's spirit pulled Becky to the house she had lived in before she died. Becky drove there, knocked on the door, asked the present occupants if she could go into the cellar, where she proceeded to have a nice long chat with her grandmother's ghost. "I had really missed her," Becky told me. "She had always encouraged me rather than lectured me, no matter what I did."

My only vision was as a seven-year-old child on my parents' last trip together, their attempt to save their marriage. We were camping in Yellowstone Park and I got the front seat of the car. In the middle of the night, I woke up to see the clouds part and Jesus holding his hands out to me. It could have been a dream, but I've never dreamed that way since, and the images are never as clear nor do they stay with me like that one did. At that moment, I felt wanted, which I must have needed with my folks fighting and all.

I never really fit in anywhere after that, so I would hang out with people like Becky, people who accepted me just the way I was, people who lived the way they wanted, people who seemed to attract lots of friends. I always wanted to be like Becky, but I was too conservative, doing all the "right" things, none of the "wrong" things. Instead of living with my boyfriend, for example, I got married at a young age. Instead of working, I stayed home with the children, even though I had trouble being alone and isolated from the world. Instead of being true to myself, I would live through the "Beckys" in my life.

Becky and I would meet at the Sundance Saloon; the band members had gone to high school with my brother. I was just an old "rock 'n' roller," I guess, trying to hang on to something I was afraid of losing—not my youth, but my rebellious nature. I had always had one, just never really exercised it before, unless you count the time I smoked Cigarellos in my basement bedroom, blowing the smoke out the window, or going to parties in high school where other people drank and smoked pot, and the worst thing I ever did was make out with my cousin's friend, who just happened to be a close friend's boyfriend.

Twenty years later, even though I was married, I wanted a boyfriend again. I wanted to know I was attractive, that had I not married at nineteen, I would have had many loves. The closest I got was a cowboy who asked me to dance and then swung me around, literally, on the dance floor. After which, he showed me his best trick—standing on his head while drinking a beer and smoking a cigarette.

My husband would join me at the Sundance sometimes on his way home from a business trip. It's a funny story, how he tells it now, but I think it hurt him, to think I wasn't happy just waiting for him while feeding the children and the fires at home. It hurt me, too, when he would call me from some noisy bar on the road, telling me how hard he was working and how much he missed me. I often wondered what he missed since when he came home we'd spend at least a day fighting, working out our roles again. I'd often escape to Becky's place by Sunday afternoon, where I would feel welcome and warm and safe.

Parties there were the best. Becky would do things like rent a hot tub. She'd invite all of her friends, as diverse as a college campus in Montana could be. With a few glasses of wine in me, I could entertain people for hours with stories about my middle class lifestyle. They especially found me fascinating the Halloween I dressed and did my hair like Mary Tyler Moore, in a little flip, the way I actually, for real, do my hair these days.

My husband dressed like a hippie that night, and we had stopped by my parents' house to get our picture taken. "Oh, you look so cute, Dianne! Just like you did in high school," my mother said. I took it as a compliment because I take what I can get. I crave attention, as I would prove when we are invited to another costume party, only at an old neighbors'.

I go as Cher, with a long black wig, and a tight short black leather skirt and a vest over my black teddy. I make the mistake of putting on my red fingernails before my fishnet stockings, so my husband has to help me with those. He goes as a sailor and carries my boombox on his shoulder, playing Cher's song, "If I Could Turn Back Time" (from her video made on a naval ship), when we ring the doorbell. No one gets it. They are all in Hawaiian shirts, like that is supposed to be a real gas in the middle of winter in Montana.

Becky was impressed with our creativity when we'd stopped by to get a temporary rose tattoo on my chest, and borrow some earrings. At the party, I begin to feel uncomfortable with all the men staring at me. I have to admit, though, I look pretty good for a mother of three who had a hysterectomy years before. We leave early, and not to waste a Saturday night out, go back to Becky's where her boyfriend has just brought back some marijuana. Honestly, I have never tried it before, but this night, dressed like I am, I forget myself and take a puff. I don't think I inhale though, as nothing happens. I watch as everyone else gets silly, knowing I'll have to drive home.

So here I am, at two in the morning, looking like Cher, driving my van through the streets of my hometown, right by my grandparents' house. "God," I think out loud, for my husband is sleeping, "wouldn't it be funny if a cop stopped me? I mean it's not even Halloween..." No, the only tickets I've gotten have been for speeding in school zones, usually going about seven miles over the limit. Even as Cher, I must look harmless and innocent. I am so boring.

Becky had taken pictures and on Monday takes one of me to our poetry teacher. "Who do you think this is?" She asks him. "Why, that's Dianne," he says, not even pausing to think about it. What kind of fantasies has he been having? It doesn't look a thing like me. I usually wear turtlenecks and sweaters, with pleated trousers, boots, and sometimes a scarf wrapped around my shoulders for warmth. Oh, yes, I also wear glasses, since I was twelve. Piercing my ears when I was twenty-five was about as Cher-like as I ever got. At a table in the cafeteria, Becky's boyfriend whispers in my ear: "You looked really good the other night. I'm having a lot of trouble in my logic class. Do you think you could help me?"

I didn't know he was after me, until he would come out to the house for a tutoring session and discover that my husband was home working, turn red, and, sweating and stammering, say he'd forgotten something else he needed to do that day. He would never need my help again, but would ask me once if I'd like to join him in his truck for a joint between classes. Years later, after I graduate and move back to Colorado, Becky kicks him out for having an affair. At that point, she calls him her husband since they basically have a common-law marriage.

So it is like another divorce for her. She has graduated from college, too, with a degree in English Literature, and is working at the Bungalow Drug behind the cash register and the lunch counter, waiting for him to finish school. It is time for her to move on to a new life, and he gives her the momentum. She plans to move back home, but not before taking a trip to Mexico with a friend. She has a short layover at the airport in Denver, so I meet her there for dinner. I've missed her, her free-flying nature. My suburban life is not in the least bit interesting.

I won't see Becky for a while, or even hear from her. She has suddenly decided to take a sojourn to Arizona to live with a friend and learn to be a travel agent. She sells her trailer and packs up her red Ford Taurus wagon for her drive alone through Idaho, Utah, and Nevada. I'm not surprised when she tells me later about the gun she kept under the seat. She is headed down the freeway in Nevada when she needs it. Two truckers surround her and motion for her to stop. She is able to load her gun, while driving, and they let her pass.

Since then, I've wanted to pack a pistol, but I don't dare, even though I can shoot a gun, having taken hunter's safety as a kid and then killing gophers in my backyard when my kids were just little. But that was in Montana where the living is a little bit easier, and it's a lot more accepted to hang your rifle in the back window of your pickup. We lived off of elk and venison, and even antelope, for a long time, until I couldn't handle the gamy smell when I was pregnant.

Becky not only knows how to shoot, she can throw knives with the best. She regularly attends Mountain Man festivals where she pitches her teepee and wears her beaded buckskin dress that she made herself. She fishes, too, as a way to unwind from a night waitressing at a fancy supper club. But that is after she comes back to Montana from Arizona. She's given up on the idea of sitting at a computer terminal all day. It just isn't in her. She has to be moving, or at least producing with words or working on a craft project or cleaning, anything.

It is back home she meets the father of her twin girls, a rodeo champion who walks into town one day, stays around long enough to get her pregnant, then disappears when she throws him out for coming home drunk one night. It is something she doesn't like in a man, and he promised her that he never drank to excess. He doesn't know she is pregnant and she will never find him, even through social services. "He has a ranch somewhere in Texas," she tells me. "And he's rich. He doesn't need to work."

Yet she needs to live in a duplex her mother owns in Billings, Montana, and she manages the rest of her mother's property there. She works at the Barnes and Noble until she goes into labor, early. The girls, she calls her twins, "visited" her in her car when she first found out she was pregnant. She had never wanted children and didn't think she could have any. So her natural response was to not have the babies, but they asked her to let them live.

So she does, almost dying in the process, having one of those out-of-body experiences in the delivery room when they take the twins by Caesarian section. "There I am," she tells me, "floating way above myself and the doctors and nurses. They are beating on my chest and I want to leave so badly. But then I think of the girls..." Which she does from then on, right up until the end, when she finally does leave...

I get a call in February when the girls are two. Becky has kidney cancer. It is a slow-growing inherited kind that she shouldn't have until her fifties. She has taken care of herself, quitting smoking, lifting weights, eating healthy. It doesn't seem fair, not now, not when she has the girls to take care of. Yet she gets on with her life, as if nothing has changed. She works part-time as a teacher's aide for the special ed class at the high school. She teaches the girls in her class to cook and sew, and takes them on outings to the park and pool, to WalMart. She takes one to a dance, on her own unpaid time, just because the girl wants to go.

Becky wants to be the best mother she can be and checks out a pile of books from the library on parenting. She knows her road is a hard one, but she doesn't in the least bit feel sorry for herself. Her back still bothers her, though, so she takes a hot bath every night after tucking the twins in bed.

It is in the tub one night that she gets a visit from the dead husband of another friend from college. He has killed himself and wants Becky to tell his wife that it wasn't her fault. It's hard for me to believe, but I believe Becky. She doesn't drink or do drugs, and she spends a lot of time meditating, candles lit on her coffee table.

I know how Becky lives as I've made a point of visiting her at least once a year when I drive through Montana visiting my relatives. I know Becky's girls at six months, at eighteen months, and then at two years after Becky has had two tumors removed from her brain, a side effect of the kidney cancer.

That summer, I go to the Women's Retreat she and her sister organize every year. I call it a powwow. The rules are simple: no men, no kids, no drugs, no booze. It is a spiritual weekend in the woods, with sharing, laughing, singing Native American songs, beating drums, and sitting around in a healing circle on Sunday morning. We lift our spirits for Becky, with faith she will be well.

But her disease spreads to her liver and lungs. I visit her the next spring, and she looks okay, but her cough keeps her from eating her breakfast when we have a chance to go out. Becky has already lived past the time the doctors had said she'd be gone. But her will is strong. She goes to a healer and follows a special diet, along with the Western doctors' regimen of drugs and therapy. She reads me my Tarot cards and my life looks good.

And my life is good. I am driving through Montana in January with my sisters, on our way to our grandma's surprise ninety-fifth birthday party. I call Becky. She can barely talk. It isn't my cell phone. "How are you?" I ask.

"Pretty good for someone in bed dying of cancer." The phone goes dead.

I call back when we get closer to town. "Yes, I want to see you," she says. "I look terrible, though."

She doesn't look terrible. She still has her long reddish hair, since her cancer is not one they attack with chemo. Her only drugs now are pain pills that make her skin itch. She is scratching her scalp so her hair is knotted up. I go to her bathroom and find her brush.

"I remember the story you wrote," I tell her, "about the old lady you took care of, who had long silver hair that you washed and brushed."

"I'd forgotten about that," she smiles. "That was a good story, wasn't it?"

"Yes, it was. It made me cry."

I stay for an hour until she sleeps. Becky dies three days later. She hasn't visited me since, although I asked her to so I can truly believe in the hereafter.

Her mother calls me several months after her death to tell me one of the girls insists that "Mommy isn't gone. She's right here with us." I believe it. Becky's last words to me were about her visit with the Grim Reaper the night before: "I'm not ready to go yet," she told him. "I have things to do. I have children to raise." And that's just what she's doing.

My Son, My Strength
by Mariah Lancaster

The box had to be just the right size, not so little that it might get lost in the postal shuffle from Maine to Louisiana, but not too big, either. I found a dusty ornament box on the top shelf of the coat closet. It was three inches square, and strong enough to carry the precious cargo. Setting it on the coffee table, I sat heavily on the couch, tired and scared.

I opened a second box, this one smaller and fancier, with a jeweler's name stamped proudly on top. My hands shook as I slipped the diamond ring off my finger and brushed my lips over its small, soft face before putting it in the box.

I missed it already, but not for sentimental reasons. It had represented the final barrier between me and the outside world, my protector from the scorn I knew I would face. Too many eyes had already slipped from my young face to my hard, round belly, to my finger. And now, my finger would be bare. I was officially alone.

In reality, I had been alone for some time. My fiancé had been discharged from the Air Force and was returning to his home state the same week I told him about the positive pregnancy test. "Don't leave me. I can't do this alone," I begged him, but he kept loading his truck, undeterred by my news.

"You know I gotta go home," he said in his dark southern voice. "But you can come with me." He spoke with confidence, knowing I wouldn't abandon college in the middle of my first semester. And so I watched him drive away, his path unaltered, while mine seemed to erode into dusty emotions and dissolving life goals.

As my son grew inside me, so did his father's indifference. For a while, I clung to the idea that we would be a family, but I soon came to my senses.

It was a gorgeous blue day when I packed up my dream of a happily-ever-after, the diamond ring, and handed it over to the protection of the post office. I was a pacing animal in a cage that had just discovered how to free itself. But now, I would *have* to take care of myself, and my son.

Caleb joined the world on a star-filled July night. I phoned his father first, but he was the last person to receive the news. While I waited for him to return my call, I apologized to the slumbering angel in my arms. "It's just you and me," I whispered. "I lost your daddy."

Yet as I held my child, I felt empowered by his small, helpless body. He was here, mine to love and to raise. I could prove to the world that I was as competent as any other mother. People would look at the pure happiness in his eyes and forgive me for bringing forth one more fatherless child, even though his father is the one who left...

The tough requirements of parenthood and school left me little time for myself, but I managed to date sporadically around toddling steps and runny noses. And each date held a new adventure. Once I came home to discover I had been sporting pureed carrots on my sleeve the entire evening. Another time, when a baby was crying in the restaurant we were having dinner, my milk let down, pooling through my red silk shirt.

I can now laugh at the night I sat huddled in the darkness of the kitchen, explaining quietly to the caller, so as not to disturb Caleb, why I didn't want to go out with him again. "Come on, now," he interrupted. "That baby needs a father, and it is your responsibility to get him one!" Thank goodness I was too busy being a mother and student to let such a remark fester in my ear.

Caleb grew strong and healthy under my love, and I, in turn, thrived on his. We had difficulties, but we faced them together. There was nothing I wouldn't do for him. No star I wouldn't pull down from the heavens, no river I wouldn't cross. But I couldn't notice that his gurgles were slow to develop, even slower to transform into words. His spectacular blue eyes, framed by extensive lashes, began to dart uncomfortably away from mine, as if it were painful for him to look at his own mother.

The doctor solidified my worries with her concern: There was something wrong with my precious baby. I fled her office as quickly as I could. In the parking lot, I wrapped my arms around Caleb, tears streaming down my cheeks onto his curly brown hair. What could I have done wrong? I never drank while I was pregnant, never allowed myself to be around cigarette smoke. I ate the right foods, took vitamins faithfully, then breast-fed Caleb until his first birthday. The only difference in his life from "normal" babies, I wrongly reasoned, was the lack of a father.

And so I found him one, in myself. I brushed up on my sporting skills, watching painfully boring football and basketball games, bypassing the educational toys in the stores and stalking paternally to the "boy" sections. I squelched my maternal side to kick balls in the park, roll trucks on the floor, and tumble roughly on the carpet.

But the barricade in front of Caleb continued to increase. By the time he was two, he had become fascinated with mechanical objects, staring obsessively into a spinning fan, for example, until I would turn it off and get his attention with something else. My "fatherly" behavior had not worked, so I returned to simply being his mother, focusing on love rather than on feminine or masculine aspects.

One day in the grocery store, I noticed the absence of condemning looks. I was explaining to Caleb the importance of comparing prices when an older couple commented on my beautiful son. Caleb was concentrating on the box of macaroni he grasped in his long fingers, but suddenly looked up, pleasing us all with the whisper of a smile.

Without thinking, I began to play with his curls as the couple and I compared notes on him and their great-grandchildren. The woman asked my advice on teething, and I provided some tips I had learned. We parted with mutual well wishes after the man planted a watery kiss on Caleb's head. My ring finger was still bare, but I realized it no longer mattered. Somehow, I had been transformed from an unwed mother, to simply a mother.

Caleb was three years old when my dearest childhood friend called. "I'm pregnant," she shivered into the receiver. I swallowed, hurting for her.

"Congratulations!" I said, meaning it. I winced when she scoffed. She was not married, and terrified to see her plans fading away.

But my plans, I told her, had not disappeared. They had simply rerouted themselves. "There is nothing wrong with having a baby on your own," I resolved, "even if you—we—are young."

I told her it wouldn't be easy, that I only discovered my capacity for extraordinary strength through raising Caleb thus far. "You have it, too," I assured her. "It will help you through this. And if I can make it," I laughed, "so can you."

In time, my friend would make an excellent single mother, and I would remarry.

My new husband was holding my hand the day a team of professionals diagnosed Caleb, then four, with autism. Even a high-functioning case was hard to accept, even though I had known something was wrong.

I also knew it wasn't the lack of a father that had hurt Caleb. In fact, I was confident I had provided him with a loving and secure environment on my own. We still have some tough obstacles in front of us, but we will face them together, and we will surpass them. We will win. Even without his new father, Caleb and I would win. We already have.

Seventh Inning Stretch
by Ann E. Byrnes

Looking back at the replay, I had the gumption of a rookie's naivete to return to the classroom after an absence of twenty years. My well-educated father teased that I was "the oldest living college freshman." But I was undaunted. Surely, if I had managed several successful career moves, the start-up of a new business, divorce after ten years of marriage, four years as a single mother, and scrambling to scrape together the funds for tuition and living expenses, being a full-time college student would be a refreshing change of pace. I was finally getting my shot at the big leagues. English 101, U.S. history, algebra, trigonometry. No sweat, I thought confidently as the line-up was announced. Easy outs.

By the end of the first week, reality deftly picked off the daring lead I was taking from the safety of my base. I became utterly overwhelmed and disheartened by it all: the incessant scheduling demands of being a full-time student and single parent of a young child, locating classrooms, uncaring professors, apathetic college kids, slogging through downpours from satellite parking lots, and having more homework than I ever imagined. Attempting to emulate the pros who indifferently chaw on a cheek-full of tobacco, I had bitten off more than I could chew. Strike one.

And then there was chemistry. The professor descended on the room in a cloud of academia almost as perceptible as the chalk dust that filled the air as he wildly wrote on the board while lecturing. He started every lesson by writing a pedantic quotation on the far chalkboard. I dutifully copied them all down, even when they made little sense to my uneducated mind. The simplest ones would read:

September 22 - The universe is full of magical things patiently waiting for our wits to grow sharper.
- Eden Philpotts

October 20 - Stupidity is a privilege of man; there is none in Nature.
- Sigismund Von Radeck

November 22 - It is a wise ignorance which knows itself.
- Blaise Pascal

The learned teacher of this class spoke of intangible matters, concepts very close to the bare truth, but invisible to the naked eye. Instead of following the slings and arrows of the game plan, my concentration stumbled. "Hey, hold on a minute," my rudimentary Galilean reasoning would interject, throwing me a bean ball. "If electrons are of insignificant mass, even on the atomic scale, how can we know so much about them...?"

My mind would be jolted back to the subject at hand by laughter, presumably at one of the instructor's antics. My attention span had balked, and by the time I thought to ask for time out to recover, the play was over. I imagined that the other twenty-nine students were uniformly nodding at every abstraction and chuckling at inside jokes, a private boys-of-summer club to which I did not belong. I thought that certainly only I conversed in Yogi-isms and was befuddled by the rapid flashing of missed signals.

Twice a week, I took my seat in the first row of sterile white countertop-desks, tiered like cheap bleachers facing a green-chalkboard playing field. The room was stark, the walls bare except for the ponderous hulk of the Periodic Table of the Elements glaring down like a masterful scoreboard, with my tally stubbornly stuck on zero.

I repeatedly peered up at this board, professed to be an awesomely systematic graphic organizer of science, nature, and mathematics, hoping to grasp some understanding of its complexities. My timing was off. When I finally located the individual box of the element being discussed, I had missed the point and fallen behind in the scoring. Like a transuranic element that has been artificially created in the laboratory, often lasting for only a fraction of a second, my comprehension was forced and fleeting.

It had been over two decades since I had last encountered these concepts, in a course called Lab Science, from which I only recalled a bespectacled high school teacher standing in front of the class, robotically demonstrating simple experiments. The playing field was different now: fast paced, competitive, computerized. I was not only twice the age of most of my teammates, I was outdated. Strike two.

The longest shadow was cast by a tall male student who always wore a Yankees' baseball cap and asked brainy, high-toned questions from his lofty perch in the top row. Like the legendary Roy Hobbs, he became a mythic figure, a supernatural icon: larger-than-life, highly scientific, and definitely out of my league. From my farm club perspective, I could only relate this classmate's façade to a character portrayed in *The Addams Family,* a television program I watched as a child.

Lurch was the formal butler for a zany family that lived in a haunted house. Outfitted in a tattered tuxedo, he was approximately nine feet tall, devoid of emotion, and humorless. Responding to the bong that beckoned him, his deep, mechanical voice intoned, "You rang?" When Lurch rolled his eyes and growled under his breath in exasperation, the sound was like the rolling thunder of an impending rainout. I secretly named the Yankee fan Lurch, and continued to be intimidated by him right down to the last class before finals.

His seeming to ace the weekly labs particularly unnerved me. These were scheduled to be three hours long, but Lurch was out of there in under two hours, tops. I always went into extra innings, the last one to finish, week after week. How I dreaded those experiments, a far cry from cookbook chemistry. We were expected to design our own procedures, write tediously detailed reports, and work independently. Teamwork was strictly discouraged, RBIs an unknown statistic.

I lamely attempted to explain the theory behind and draw conclusions from investigations that confounded me. The assignments weighed as heavily on my mind as the thick textbook that saddled me as I toted it in my book bag. That book weighed 2267.98785 grams. I know. I weighed it on the electronic balance. It was probably the only accurate measurement I took for months, which was how long I took to get out of the greenhorn's bullpen of mis-measuring my meniscus.

It seemed as if I committed a bungling error on every play. The demands of the course were dizzying, my head spinning with memorization of definitions, scientific laws, nomenclature, significant figures, formulas, dimensional analysis, calculations, oxidation states, and reactions, all jumbled together like haphazard play diagrams tumbling from their easel as fast as I could upright them. H.J. Dutiel once said that baseball is "a game which consists of tapping a ball with a piece of wood, then running like a lunatic." I was definitely in the bush leagues of hit and run.

We took the first exam in the lab, a cold and ominous room with black, aseptic benches. It smelled ever-faintly of compounds made from manipulating the elements. Inescapably, the menacing statistics of the Periodic Table dictated the play-by-play of this test of skill. True to form, Lurch completed his work in under an hour, while I frantically rushed to finish within the allotted two hours. Instead of choking up, I simply choked.

Could I actually make practical use of Avogadro's Number, chemistry's base unit? Would I remember how to use the endless conversion factors? And where to begin on question #7, which read: *The atomic weight of gold is 196.97. If you were offered an atomic weight of gold for one dollar, would you buy it? Why or why not? Explain completely.* Could I possibly bluff my way through this contest?

I could not. When the eight-page test was handed back, mine was hopelessly scrawled with the red ink of corrections. I had been tagged out sliding into first base, the wind knocked out of me. I was a straight-A student. I did not get "71's." And there was no curve to this pitch; this was a "D" on the rigid grading scale of the class. I was crushed. Strike three.

I felt like the batter who strikes out after having waited out the count to no strikes, and three balls, with the score 4-0 and the bases loaded in the bottom of the ninth inning. I took little notice that one-third of the class had dropped out from the line-up. I resolutely refused to be defeated by a losing season. Determined not to be brushed back by an inside fastball, I steadfastly dug myself deeper into the batter's box.

That "71" and I faced off. Desperately trying to drum knowledge into my hard head, I pestered the professor, the lab technician, other students, strangers in the library, until I gleaned every answer. When I did not understand the solution I wrote down clues to its explanation. When I did not understand the clues, I researched them. When I did not understand the research, I sometimes cried before returning to the dogged pursuit of my precious little victories.

As classes progressed, so did my realization that I need not stand stranded out in left field futilely squinting into the glaring sun of the unknown. The instructor, the drillmaster on this playing field, often exasperated me by refusing to act as a designated hitter, answering my endless questions with ones of his own, smiling impishly and simply saying, "I can't tell you that," or wordlessly watching while we goofed up our lab experiments.

Over time, though, he proved to be approachable and willing to accommodate those who reached out for help. When I did, I was offered more than academic coaching. Just as important was the cheering in the form of encouragement and support while I ran a difficult baseline. Slowly I began to relax as I came out from the dugout to take my turn at bat.

I survived the contenders of melting points, density measurements, specific heat, metathesis, and kinetics. Somewhere around acid-base titrations and determination of the identities of unknown compounds, little flashes of understanding began to ignite. Recognizing that switch hitters stay in the game, I struggled to upgrade my abilities, to adapt, to check my swing, and to learn from my mistakes. I achieved a good eye for accuracy in measurements, and became otherwise quite adept in the lab. It was marvelous and scary at the same time.

Although I spent endless, halting hours taking batting and fungo practice, I became my own winning relief pitcher instead of a catcher without a mask. Once when I mustered the courage to ask a question about the excess products in an equilibrium equation, the professor actually said to the class, "Now, listen to what she's asking. It's a good question." I laughed at the right times during the lectures, and even understood most of the signals that Lurch sent through his cross examinations (which I began vaguely to suspect correlated to slick spitballs).

And so it was with a feeling of great accomplishment, having striven and prevailed in my run down with the science god, that I received a perfect score on the last test of the semester. Written with a bold green stroke was *100*, and in one corner a few words of congratulations from the taskmaster I had once been sure would bench me for life: *This is really good work, Ann!* Pulling out of a long, wearisome slump, I had ended with a batting average over .300. At that moment I did not feel like the losing side of a shut out. The struggling, frustration, and intimidation that had been required for the victory suddenly seemed more than a sacrificial pop fly. Despite my stumbling, grappling form, I had learned in this class that no-hitters are accomplished one batter at a time.

Then Lurch lumbered down to the chalkboard to discuss the test with the instructor. I overheard him comment offhandedly that a "C" would satisfy the requirements of his major. I craned my neck to sneak a glance at his test paper and its wide green mark at the top: *73*.

I was flabbergasted. A revelation sparked in my mind as bright as the glaring light towers of a night game. My trepidation had been largely groundless. For the first time, I saw this student, not as Roy Hobbs, superstar, but as the tall-but-ordinary young man that he was. His grumblings had been ones of puzzlement similar to my own.

Moreover, rather than trying to knock one out of the park, he was satisfied to advance on balls or stolen bases. In my eyes, the giant fell in one swift stroke. Like the natural phenom who in the crucial moment falls from grace, the image of his looming figure, crumpled on the ground, was at once frightening, strangely endearing, and indelibly marked in my memory.

A Lesson from Paris
by Lisa Minassian

"What do you want to be when you grow up?" my cousin, Tanya, asked.

"I don't know. Maybe a veterinarian. All I know is *I want to go to Paris...*"

In the middle of college, I left to join the Marine Corps and ended up on Parris Island for three months before being sent to Okinawa for a year.

In letters home to Boston, I wrote, *I finally made it to Paris, but there's no Eiffel Tower here. There are barracks, rifle ranges, and bellowing drill instructors. I think I made a wrong turn.*

My plans to make it to Paris had gone awfully awry.

Following my discharge, I finished college and my roommates and I spoke of how we'd go to Europe after graduation. But once we graduated, we had to find "real jobs." I worked as a counselor for troubled adolescents, kids who were taken from their families or had emotional problems. I loved it. I felt it was my calling, that I actually made a difference in the teens' lives. But something was still missing. Every day, I still dreamed of going to Europe and setting foot in France.

After six months, I saw an ad for Eurobus, a very inexpensive way to travel through Europe. "I'm going to Europe this spring. Whoever wants to can come with me," I announced to my friends.

No volunteers stepped forward. I waited until the last second of the deadline then ran to the post office to mail my check in time. That was it; I was going.

I had to sidestep the issue around my father, who is of a strict Armenian background where women don't travel alone. I even avoided telling my mother who was English and would understand my urge to travel. She visited the U.S. as a teenager, and after falling in love with my father, ended up staying in the States.

I had no one else to keep me home. The last few years, I had avoided relationships with men. While in high school and college, I had a volatile, tempestuous, and unhealthy one. I was fed up with the fights and the jealousy. Each time my friends reported another problem with their men, I was relieved to be "single." I had plans to travel, ideas to try; I wouldn't be kept back by a man.

My girlfriend, Zepure, took me to the airport after a farewell with my other friends at our favorite Boston pub.

At the gate I confessed, "I'm kind of scared."

"Lisa, you've been talking about Paris ever since I met you. You'll be fine. You'll have such a wonderful time that you probably won't want to come back."

"I'm not sure I want to leave."

"Go on. Everything will be the same when you get back. Nothing's going to change here..."

The first few days in London were terrible, and I wanted to go home right away. I was jetlagged and had caught a terrible cold on the plane. I found little pleasure taking in the sights of the rainy, foggy city where my mother had grown up.

Finally, I boarded the overnight bus to Paris. We transferred to a ferry at Dover, and as the white cliffs disappeared into the horizon, I reveled in the idea that soon I'd be in Calais, France, and shortly after that—Paris.

"Un café, s'il vous plait," I almost exclaimed at a rest stop, uttering my first French words on French soil. The words "I'm in France, I'm in France" danced in my head as I scanned my surroundings and understood some of the signs, courtesy of my high school French class. A couple of hours later, we were in Paris.

I stepped off the bus and wandered away from the rest of the travelers, content just to walk and breathe in the city. Every step felt unbelievable. And yet, it was nothing like I expected.

It was cold and rainy, and I had no place to go. Most everything was closed, the only illumination coming from street lamps and Metro signs. After a couple of hours, my backpack had grown very heavy. I looked for an inexpensive hotel but couldn't find anything.

I couldn't figure out the phones, which took phone cards instead of money, and I had to search for one that accepted francs. I called the nearest youth hostel, and they were completely booked. Now I had no money left for the Metro; I had to find some place and soon.

I walked some more, kicking myself for not being prepared. At a police station, I asked in my horrible French for directions to the youth hostel. Even if it was full, I was so desperate that I planned to beg for a patch of land to pitch my tent. I walked for another half hour.

The Auberge de Jeunesse D'Artagnan turned out to be a gaudy, green-trimmed building, very unlike the brilliant, beautiful architecture in the rest of the city. They had no spare ground to pitch anything on. I went in not knowing what else to do.

A sign at the reception desk read, *Waiter/waitress wanted for two weeks in exchange for room and board.*

I had no experience and no working papers, and spoke little French, but I was desperate. When the man in front of me asked about the job, my heart sank. He turned it down when he realized it paid nothing. I took my chances.

Next thing I knew, I was in my own room overlooking Paris—for free. I spent the next day exploring the city. I finally achieved the pinnacle that truly meant *I was actually there* by climbing the Eiffel Tower. I was the luckiest woman alive. If I never accomplished anything in my life, at least this dream had finally come true.

Then I met Cyril, head chef of the restaurant. I could barely breathe. He had the most sultry, incredible French accent, a tall, broad physique, sandy brown hair and a strong jawline. I thought I would drop my tray every time I walked by him. He followed me with his eyes and I thought he was going to criticize me or even fire me—what did I know about being a waitress? It took a few days before I realized he was interested in *me*.

We small-talked in my terrible French and his broken English, but mostly made eye contact and flirted. By day we worked together; by night we hung out with locals downstairs in the bar and met people from around the world. We spent time in city parks holding hands. One day as we walked around the lake at Vincennes, he pulled me into his arms and kissed me. Then he whispered into my ear, "I love you."

I was puzzled. "Do you mean that you like me?"

"No, love," he answered. "Not like, I love you."

What could be better—I was in Paris and in love. It was like something out of the movies.

"I love you, too."

All too soon, my two weeks were up and it was time for me to move on. As we drank wine in the bar, talking of life, Marie, another French co-worker, said, "Don't go. You can stay here with us. Work here, we need somebody."

Cyril's eyes brightened, "Yes, stay here with me."

I was so thrilled to hear this. Maybe this was more than just a two-week fling to him. And I could live here, live in Paris.

"No, I can't. I only have two months to see all of Europe. I *have* to go..."

I left on a Saturday after a bittersweet farewell. I was miserable thinking of Cyril, thinking of Paris, on every bus ride, in every museum, through every city. Places like Salzburg momentarily distracted me, but nothing could compare to Paris. I longed to go back.

In Budapest, I could afford to live like a queen and not a starving traveler. Yet everywhere I went, there were references to Paris, and I started to become homesick, not for Boston, but for Paris and the life I had established there. I heard Edith Piaf in a restaurant and shortly after saw *Sabrina* in which the heroine goes off to Paris and grows to her potential in the city of lights. I was hit by a revelation—"I can go to Paris *right now.*"

In a frenzy, I rushed back to the campground where I was staying. It was late and I got lost. I wandered down residential streets and startled one dog that began barking, setting off other dogs until it seemed all the dogs in Budapest were barking at me. When I found the campground, the gates were locked, and I had to scale the fence, ripping one of my two pairs of jeans. I grabbed my bags and rushed to catch the last bus. I missed it and hailed a cab.

"I need to go to the airport," I signaled.

It was after midnight when the cab dropped me off. The airport was closed until the morning. A security guard approached me. "What are you doing here?" he asked.

"I'm trying to catch a plane to Paris."

"You are at the wrong airport; this is the *cargo* airport." Just as I thought my plan was failing, he said, "I'll call another cab for you."

I barely had enough Hungarian currency to pay the driver, and then the passenger airport was also closed. Now I was freezing out on a curb all night, all alone, with no money.

Two Dutchmen came up to me a few minutes later. "Damn communism," the dark one muttered. "Are you waiting for the airport to open, too?"

"Yes, I just got here."

"Don't stay out here and freeze," he said sympathetically. "You can wait in our car."

I was wary, but it was so cold, I took him up on it.

After only a fitful few minutes of sleep that night, we wished each other well, and I rushed to the AirFrance counter. "I need one ticket to Paris, please..."

A few hours later, I was back in Paris. Then I felt stupid. I had told the people at the hostel that I wouldn't be back for another month or so. Since there was no guarantee I'd get my job back, I went to a nearby hotel. They offered me a job handing out flyers to people who took the trains into Paris. I did it for one day and hated it. I decided to return to the hostel and my French-American romance.

Weeks later, Cyril and I were at work when suddenly he looked horrified. "My girlfriend is here!"

"Girlfriend? *Girlfriend!*" Everything went black. A woman with long, dark hair, smooth white skin, and glasses walked in with two older women.

"That's my girlfriend. We live together," he said, visibly shaken.

I had to *wait* on my boyfriend's girlfriend. As I was taking their order, she smiled and pointed to Cyril. "That is my future husband," she said, practicing her English on me.

Everything started spinning. Was I a fool, an idiot not to have seen this? Damn Frenchmen! I should have known better. How could I have been so prudent for so long and then fallen into a situation like this? I wanted to hit him, tell her the truth about Cyril and me and walk out of there forever. But then I'd lose it all because of him—my job, my place, and my dream.

I kept my cool for the rest of the evening, counting the minutes until the nightmare would end. I wasn't going to let him ruin everything.

The next day I confronted him. "Are you living with that girl? Are you going to marry her?"

"Yes," he said. "I love you. But I love her, too."

"That's ridiculous. How can you love us both?"

"It's true. I love you both the same. But I'm going to marry her."

"Then it's over. I'll not be second-best to anyone," and I walked out with my head held high.

Luckily, my friend, Zepure, was visiting and helped me with the breakup. We went to a café and drank cognac and cried and laughed about the whole mess.

"Lisa, I don't think you ever really loved him. You're in love with *Paris*. That's why you're here, that's why you came back. It's the city, it's not him."

I considered what she said for a minute. The wound was too fresh for her words to register, but I did let them roll around in my head.

It was difficult for Cyril and me to continue working together. My co-workers still rooted for the romance. Marie said more than once, "I know he loves you, Lisa, and he wants to be with you. But he lives in *her* house; she has money. You know how it is."

Yeah, I knew how it was all right. I was willing to sacrifice it all—to leave my home, my family, my country—to start a new life here. And he wasn't willing to do anything, except lie back comfortably and play us both.

There were a few times I almost fell for his continued wooing. But then I'd loathe myself for starting to cave. "I am just a toy to him." Each day we argued a bit more until we eventually fought over everything. One night, I stormed out of the hostel, paced the streets, and tortured myself for letting him affect me so much. In my confused rage, I was oblivious to the Parisians spilling out of the cafés with their characteristic *joie de vivre*.

Suddenly, I caught the reflection of the lampposts glistening in the puddles of the cobblestone streets. And then it didn't matter. Why care about this silly romance? I was in Paris, living out my dream. Paris was immense, full of opportunities. The best thing to do was to escape this draining relationship.

I found a new home and job as an au pair for a nice Canadian family in the heart of Montmartre, the Paris you see in paintings, with sidewalk cafés and street performers, atop a hill overlooking the rest of the city. I began to recognize people on the tiny streets, giving me a sense of community.

I wasn't partying with an international crowd anymore, but I found contentment living alone in my own studio. I did things I had always wanted to do—taught myself how to cook, read all the books I wanted to read, wrote about my travels. Montmartre was what I needed. I felt my soul healing there and peace, really, for the first time in my life.

I called home: "Zepure, remember when you said I probably didn't really love Cyril, that I was just in love with Paris? I think you were right. I was so deliriously fascinated by the city my first few days here that I probably transferred those feelings to the first guy I met, wishing for a

French-American romance. Thank God, I left to explore Europe back then. I'm so glad I didn't throw it away for a fantasy."

I soon realized it was time to go home. I returned back to Boston, my family, and friends. A few months later, I saw a for-sale ad for a bookstore north of Boston. In high school, I had worked in a used bookstore and thought, "One day, I'll own my own store."

As soon as I walked in, I fell in love with the place. There were five different rooms in a horseshoe shape: a children's room with birds, a tea room with tables, a room full of gifts, a room with new books, and one with used ones. I wanted to blurt out, "I'll buy it," but thought that for once in my life I shouldn't be so spontaneous. So I had my parents come look at it with me.

My mother felt the same way I did about the store. "You're an adult, you make your decisions, and we'll support you."

My father couldn't understand. "Why don't you go and get a real job and put your degree to some use, get benefits." Sensible, yes, but I didn't follow his advice. I bought Chapter One Book Shoppe and dug myself in. It was a lot harder than I ever imagined. I spent the first year working long hours while I learned about the business. I never had time to read anymore.

I've been happy ever since, satisfied with my lifestyle and writing about what I've experienced. Now I understand why I had to leave Paris— my "true love" was waiting for me all along here in Boston. But I never would have known had I not followed my dream.

A House of Her Own
by Dianne Lorang

Even though she works in Montana for a while with my husband, I don't meet Nancy until we both live in Colorado toward the end of 1993, at a Halloween party where my husband and I go as the two female Supreme Court judges—I as Sandra Day O'Connor and he as Ruth Bader Ginsberg. I wear my graduation gown from just a few years ago and he wears our oldest daughter's from high school (complete with pantyhose and size 10 black pumps from Payless Shoes).

I am almost forty and Nancy is around thirty, single, fun, friendly, and, to say the least, animated. She practically lives out of her old Subaru wagon as that is where she keeps her mountain bike, inline skates, skis (both downhill and cross-country), hiking boots, backpack, sleeping bag, tent, and much of the assorted outdoor clothing she has collected by moonlighting at a sporting goods store. Her day job is a geologist with my husband's mining company.

Everyone likes Nancy, always including her on guest lists for parties. She stays with our children once when we go away for the weekend, and we have her over for Thanksgiving dinner. I have a single sister in town so it makes for an even number around the table, which is stupid, I know, but then I'm a product of society.

We go out with Nancy and other couples to "happy hours," dinner, brunch on Sunday, and even, for a while, the local university for ice-skating on the hockey rink. This proves harder to schedule since the hours are on weeknights and a lot of our friends travel for business. Even Nancy does. I'm not that important. Although I work some, I'm basically "just a housewife," a kept woman.

Nancy and I become enthusiastic members of the company mountain bike team. We train a lot as a group before riding thirty miles on forest trails and old logging roads just to camp out and get a free tee-shirt and a massage, for a good cause, though. We've all raised pledges and have no idea what agony we're in for. Through it all, Nancy and I become good friends. I tell her almost everything.

We share an ongoing tragedy in that her superior has gotten very ill and the doctors cannot diagnose him. He's in and out of hospitals while his wife copes with living in a new place, having also just moved from

Montana, and four young children, one who is ill herself with some strange malady, different but similar to her father's. He will die in a year and a half of Creutzfeldt-Jacob disease (CJD)[6], which will only be confirmed by an autopsy.

It is when he is very ill and it is all I can do to be an understanding friend and babysitter to his soon-to-be widow, that I lean on Nancy more and more for support. I'm having problems with work, my husband, my teenagers, myself. Nancy's apartment in Denver is an easy place to escape to in the evenings or on weekends. Before we know it, it is another spring and time to train for another grueling bike ride in the mountains.

But this time, something is wrong with Nancy's back. She spends the weekend bumming painkillers, which she has never needed much of before, and finding ice to put on her lower back. She can't finish the ride and has to take the sag-wagon back to base camp, which is almost humiliating for her. Yet she doesn't complain and joins us for our celebration dinner.

The doctors can't find much wrong, so she starts physical therapy and ends up, in the months to come, getting acupuncture and going through a series of rolfing sessions, an intense type of massage. But that is after she starts to lose her balance. She can no longer trust herself to drive so rides the diesel-drenched bus that takes an hour or more just to catch another bus to work. She doesn't live close to anyone at work, since they all live in nice houses in the suburbs and she lives more in the city, because it's cheaper.

She goes to doctor after doctor after doctor and finally learns to use the Internet where she finds out she has the same symptoms as people with Lyme disease, which is an East Coast ailment carried by deer ticks. Then she remembers the conference she attended in Pennsylvania where she took a walk in the woods and lay down to take a nap. It's been almost a year ago at this point, and she doesn't remember getting a bite or circular rash of any kind. She didn't know to look for such signs.

She finds a specialist in Steamboat Springs, Colorado. Even though it's too late to treat her with the usual antibiotics that abate Lyme disease in the early stages, he puts her on very potent ones intravenously. A nurse comes to her apartment every day. Nancy's not working now and fortunately drawing extended sick pay and has decent medical insurance. Still, it's difficult for someone with her previous lifestyle to be not only

---

[6] More widely known as mad cow disease.

inactive but alone most of the time. She gets depressed and has to go on yet more medication, which messes with her metabolism.

Her financial situation forces her to move to a smaller apartment up the street and we all pitch in. She seems okay, not wanting to burden anyone with how bad it really is. I visit her on my own, but usually when I'm lonely and wanting an outlet. Not very thoughtful, I know, but I'm one of those immature middle-aged women. I do know how awful it is to be dizzy and nauseated, though, and depressed, as I've had my bouts with such things, just not for as long as Nancy. And mine went away. Nancy's doesn't.

She tries to return to work for a while but can't do it, physically or mentally. She goes on permanent disability. She can no longer afford to live on her own and has to go stay with her mother in a condo community in Florida. We stay in touch by e-mail, though most of her letters are simply about her progress. Her life has become communicating with other "Lymies" online and learning all she can to get well.

She goes in for oxygen chamber treatments, takes a lot of supplements, and spends time sitting in the pool and sun. She does not have the stamina to swim. Some days are better than others, but not much changes for several years.

I haven't heard from her for some time, and am wondering why, when I get an e-mail from her from Butte, Montana. She has suddenly moved back there, well enough to be on her own again! My husband visits her first during a business trip. She owns her own little house on the hill above the Berkeley Pit, the ghastly hole left by the Anaconda copper mining operation. Other scars are evident in Butte, such as poverty and alcoholism and family violence, but it feels like home to Nancy, especially since she can afford one there.

Her house is a turn of the century place that needs a lot of work. But she's game and it fits into her life of selling magazine ads using her computer and fax machine. My husband tells me I'd be jealous as I've always wanted a little cozy place of my own in a community like Butte, just not Butte.

Perhaps my prejudice comes from my great-grandfather dying from too many pints in a flophouse there. I'm from a different kind of town in Montana, more of a white-collar place. Shortly after my husband's visit, we get a postcard of Nancy sitting on her front porch railing, looking oh so healthy and slim, her dark brown hair as thick and shiny as ever. The blue

Montana sky, as blue as the trim around the door, is reflected in the thick wavy (from age) window behind her. I can't wait to go there.

And so I do, last winter. She fixes me and my two sisters and youngest daughter homemade chicken soup. It's a perfect Sunday night meal as we're all fighting off colds. We're on our way home after surprising our grandma for her ninety-fifth birthday in Missoula, Montana. It's raining, a strange weather phenomenon for January in Montana. But we can only smile.

"So how did you get well?" I ask. "You look so good. Better than before you were sick."

"Divine intervention," she answers, telling us about the cranial osteopath whose treatments were 100 percent "laying on of the hands. I stopped taking drugs and started meditating. I took Tai Chi for my balance. I prayed."

We barely have time to eat, take snapshots of Nancy and me, and then take the grand tour of her house. She has an old-fashioned gas stove, a modern fridge from Scandinavia, and an antique claw-foot bathtub. She's refinished the hardwood floors but has no furniture in the parlor, nor a television. It is all still in storage in Denver. A guitar leans in a corner and one potted plant thrives in the other.

Nancy has added funky linoleum in her attic office where a cot adorns one wall, ready for passing guests. I hope to sleep there next time I'm through town, for I'm usually on my own traveling the "homeland," taking my time, driving under the speed limit, which Montana has again after not having for a year or so.

I have my chance in July. I've been to a wedding in Great Falls and to Missoula to see Grandma. It's a Monday evening and Nancy steers me to her home via my cell phone. Her neighborhood looks so different during the day without dirty slush pushed up against every curb. I'm looking forward to dinner at the Uptown Café.

She has company, which is no big surprise. Another friend is passing through and has already snagged the cot. I don't really mind. I can simply travel on that night to Bozeman where another bed awaits me. Dinner is good, and I get to practice my listening skills rather than just talking about me. Nancy went skiing last winter and rode her bike some this summer, on the path around town where the railroad used to run. She even had a long-distance boyfriend for a while.

I leave around 8:00, an hour or so before sundown, so I can get over Homestead Pass while there is still a view. As I drive into the Gallatin

Valley on the other side, the forest fires that will make Montana a national disaster area in a few months have just started. It is smoky and my eyes burn. But the fires turn the sunset a gorgeous red.

I recall Nancy's eyes sparkling at her front gate as she looked out over the pit left by the miners. She doesn't mind the hole that is now filling up with poisonous water. She used to be a miner of sorts herself. She knows she can help clean up the pit. She's already started by joining the 100-woman choir that sang and danced for its recovery.

Such a miracle, such an endeavor, is easy in her mind. After all, she's already overcome a much more potent personal pollution. And even though she'll never be the person she once was (she'll always have to pace herself), she has become an even better person. More fun, friendly, and, yes, even more animated.

Tightwired
by Sharon Eberhardt

I sat gripping the edge of the table for stability, fighting nausea as always. In the far corner, the doctors were discussing my case. The little group broke up and the ear specialist walked over and smiled as he hunkered down.

"What you have, Mrs. Eberhardt, is something called bilateral vestibular neuritis. In simple terms, you have only ten percent balance in the left ear and none at all in the right. You'll need to learn to balance all over again. There are exercises..."

"Are you telling me this won't ever go away? That I won't ever be able to work again?" I heard my voice rise over the buzzing tinnitus in my head, my heart pounding like a hammer in panic.

"I cannot live like this. *No one* can live like this!" I started to cry. "I have a husband in the hospital, a teenage daughter."

I'd been given the death sentence. For nine long months, I'd had this disabling vertigo, inability to think, interruptions in fine motor control. There were times I could not even crawl to the bathroom before throwing up.

Now sobbing, I said, "I can't even walk straight. There must be something more you can do for me."

"Time is the best healer, Mrs. Eberhardt. Time and patience."

I would have laughed if not for the nausea welling up inside me. Didn't these doctors know that this condition took your ability to even think? As if some giant black spider was forcing its way into your brain and stirring it up with poisonous legs like a batch of bad soup? Did they understand that you cannot tell your left from your right, even in your own home? This was not just dizziness that one gets at a carnival. This was an upside-down world of hell, a twilight zone of waves and movement, the sound of screeching train brakes constantly running through your head.

I cried all the way home with my one remaining friend, Helen, at my side. Not only was she my friend, but my wheels, for I could no longer drive. She dropped me off at home, making sure I was in the door, not falling off the porch as I had in the past.

"How on earth will I care for John now?" I thought. The tears burned my eyes. I surveyed the scrap of paper from the doctor with its diagrams

93

of different head movements. I staggered over to the refrigerator and fixed it there with a magnet.

I lay my head as still as possible on the couch as I remembered the day my mother signed my marriage license. I had bounced up the stairs to our apartment in Brantford, Ontario, the smell of my twin baby brothers drifting down the stairs to greet me. He was standing there, this monstrous man. He had asked for my hand in marriage, and she had given it. I froze in fear as I watched the two of them drinking together. She knew he would use me, beat me, torture me, yet she still signed me away like a rag doll. I never said "no" to Mother. I knew to "mind my elders," including this evil man who would be my first husband.

I ran away after five long years in a harsh cold place called Newfoundland. I could not abide the cruelty, the poverty, anymore. I scrimped and saved until I had enough boat fare to make my way home. I cried when I got off of the boat, kneeling down and kissing the cool sidewalk. I had never thought I would be free again. I was twenty-one.

A year later I met the man who would father my one and only child. My daughter was three when I realized he was having an affair with a fourteen-year-old. "I love you, Sharon, but I need an open window," he confessed.

"I'll do you one better," I said, hiding the pain in my chest. "I'll give you an open door!" I swung it wide for him and he took it, walking out of our lives forever. I vowed never to love again.

I was a waitress with an eleventh-grade education, and I wanted to become a nurse. The government was offering free courses, but there was a two-year waiting period. "I'm going to Edmonton to see my boyfriend," my little sister told me one day. "There's no waiting period there. Why don't you come with me?"

Life in that cold monetary city proved tough. For the first year, my daughter, Ravonna, rode the bus to school with me. But the second year, during the practical part of my training, I was on all three shifts at the hospital. I did not trust my daughter to strangers, so I took her back to Ontario to live with my older sister. I cried all the way back to Edmonton. We had never been apart for more than a day before.

As soon as I graduated, with honors, I rushed back to Ontario, where I gathered Ravonna into my arms, found a job, and made a home for us. I worked hard, only dating on and off, not trusting men. I raised my girl. I spent most of my free time with her. We would set aside time for ourselves, once a week. We would go out to a restaurant, then take in the latest movie. We read books together. I was not looking for anyone special in my life. I had all I wanted.

Then one day I met a gentleman in the hospital. A strong-willed, blue-eyed soul whom I would marry. He walked with a slight limp and used a cane. "Colleen (he always used my middle name), I have MS. Does this bother you?" he asked one day. I put my arms around him for my answer. I felt safe with John.

John declined swiftly after our marriage. He went from cane to scooter to a big ugly black wheelchair in a matter of two years. He needed hospitalization, and I brought him home on weekends and holidays. The MS struck his eyesight, his bladder and bowel functions, and totally paralyzed everything except his right arm. Even his speech became incoherent at times. His mind, however, remained sharp. The disease robbed him of everything except this and his love for me.

We all coped together until one day when I was sitting at my sister's place, drinking tea. I felt an enormous pressure build up in my head. I tried to rise from my chair, but fell instead. My daughter's boyfriend drove me to the clinic. A weary, over-worked doctor diagnosed me with a simple inner ear infection. "Take these antibiotics," he said. "It will be gone in two weeks." I was not worried.

It did not, however, go away. I could not keep the antibiotics down when I went home. I clung to the couch in a whirlwind of movement. Ravonna took over the chores in the house, even the cooking. The smell of food would trigger the nausea and I would stagger, seldom making it to the bathroom, the vomit projecting out through my fingers. My eyes could not focus on anything anymore. Everything was in constant movement. Up and down. Up and down. Spinning, whirling. Even sleep was no escape.

The noise grew louder at night, blocking all else out. I woke up screaming, falling. I could not dress myself. Creeping around the house like some kind of wounded animal, day after day I wore the same outfit. It was black. I did not notice or care until Ravonna asked, "Can you wear something else, Mom? I need to do the wash."

The doctor told me to concentrate on the radio. The brain would adjust. I did not understand because of the searing earaches. A hot lead wire pushed and shrieked through my head. Again and again. Night after night. The days scattered through a maze of insanity. I wanted to die.

I did not stop visiting John at the hospital, although the three-block walk seemed like miles. One day I heard a loud blast from a horn. The driver hung his head out of the window. "Stupid broad!" he screamed.

"Get out of the way!" I realized I had wandered, cane and all, into the middle of the road. He had missed me by inches.

My neighbors watched me coming and going. They, too, visited John. One told him, "Your wife has taken to drinking, you know." It was time to tell John what the doctors had said, that I had permanently lost my balance.

"No, Colleen, no." His face strained with emotion. "That means I can't come home anymore. I'm ill enough for the both of us." His pale sallow skin reddened with anger, hurt.

"I can't help it," I sobbed. "It might get better. I've been doing these silly head exercises." I remembered the last time John had come home. While frying us some dinner, I reached for the spatula in the pan and bumped it instead, spilling grease all over the red hot burner. A whoosh of flame, and the pan and stove were on fire. I doused them with baking soda, but when the Red Cross came to take John back to the hospital, they saw the damage.

"This is *not* good," the driver lectured. "You're a nurse. You should know the danger you're putting him in." He was right. I couldn't have gotten John out of the house if it had caught on fire. He was six feet, four inches. I was a mere five feet and weighed 106 pounds.

After that, I was never alone with my husband again. We would always have a chaperone of sorts, someone in the house within hearing distance. We had laughed at the fire, but we didn't laugh about it now.

"I want to buy a new house, Colleen," John said. "I think we need a different environment. I can get a volunteer. I want a big kitchen, one I can roll around in. And birds. I want lots of birds."

I didn't go house hunting for two years, and then only on my good days. Ravonna had married her boyfriend by then, and they helped me in my search. "It has everything you want," I told John, "plus it's right by the river. Our son-in-law is building a ramp for you as we speak."

John only spent that one summer with me. We would sit in the backyard, the smell of roses permeating the afternoon heat, the call of birds cackling and twirping at the new brand of seeds I had put out for them. The first time John saw a bluejay, his eyes grew huge, matching the color of the feathers on the bird.

"A yellow canary! Colleen, did you see that?" He sounded like an excited schoolboy, not even knowing the name of the bird he had seen. I served him cool lemonade, and we sipped from the same straw. We were children, and this backyard was our private paradise.

Then fall came and with it the cold season. Each cold John caught attacked his lungs more violently than the last. Helen drove me to the hospital so I could read to him. My awkward words made him smile. One day the floor was short-staffed, and John needed changing. I tackled the job only to put the Attends on backwards. I broke out in tears. John laughed. He laughed so hard that I laughed, too.

"Oh, you and your upside-down brain have done it again, Colleen!" After that, we used humor and laughter to make it through the pain.

It was the first day of spring. I had the strangest phone conversation with John. "I'm worried," he said. "Will you always be here for me, Colleen?"

"I'm not going anywhere. Are *you* going somewhere?" I joked. With that, he laughed and hung up. Ten minutes later, the hospital called. "Come up now, John has aspirated."

I rushed, getting dizzy as usual, and confused. The nurses clustered around him. My spine bristled. My mouth went dry. The room started whirling. "It's time to say good-bye," I thought.

I held him one last time. "It's all right, John," I said in a calm voice. "This body does not want you anymore." His face relaxed, and he died minutes later. We had been married for less than six years. We both were forty-seven.

I was to become sicker even though I thought I had been through the worst. I was alone, with no one to confide in except Helen, and Ravonna whom I didn't want to bother as she was going through a difficult pregnancy.

"She did this to herself," my family would whisper. "Marrying a man who she knew had MS. She always takes on too much." The days and nights became as one. I staggered and inched my way through the months. The tinnitus, which had subsided to a bearable degree, came in like a roaring lion, the noise intolerable. My daughter suggested my getting a boarder. I refused.

There were days when I could not see, my vision blurred by the ever-moving aquarium that had become my world. The smell of food, coffee, cigarettes, even the copper pipes in the bathroom would waft into my nostrils, filling my mouth with a pungent taste, soon followed by bile.

I opened the refrigerator door, and a kaleidoscope of color and odor assaulted my senses. I fell backwards, hitting the floor with a resounding thud. The cupboard was a confused jumble. Totally meaningless to me. Nothing made sense. I did not recognize myself when I peered into the mirror. I opened the door, and a cool breeze drifted in, letting me know that summer had not yet arrived.

One day my eyes were so misty that I reached in my handbag and took out Anbesol. I read the label three times as a good nurse does. It said *for toothache*. My brain read *eyes*. I tipped the little tube and realized too late that the gel was not the consistency it should have been. The powerful drop hit my eye dead center, almost blinding me.

Ravonna and my granddaughter were with me. "Mom, what are you doing?" I didn't care. My emotions had dissipated somewhere in this twirling mirage my life had become, abandoning me totally one day when I had actually fallen off the toilet.

Ravonna insisted I go back to the doctors. They tried anti-depressants, which made things worse. I lost my depth perception. My granddaughter looked small and flat. I dared not pick her up. I knew I would drop her. There were tests and more tests. MRIs, CT scans, and one nasty little thing called an ENG, pouring warm and cool water in the ear canal and measuring the patient's eye movements. The little piece of nerve that was left had died.

They found a lesion on the frontal lobe of my brain, not unlike that of MS. Nothing more. The doctors shook their heads.

I gripped the refrigerator and cast my eyes up toward the crucifix hanging on the wall. It moved in ever-increasing spirals. "If you are going to allow a stroke or an aneurysm, then get on with it!" I screamed into the silence of the house. No answer. I felt anger surge. Emotion for the first time in months. "You are my Father! I am Your child! You know me! I want answers!"

A few days later, Helen suggested I buy a computer, get online, and research my dreadful condition. I came across an Internet support group called *Dizzinews*. I wrote them and they accepted me as a long-lost member of their family. I was no longer alone in my illness. One member mentioned a treadmill as the best medicine for this disease. It didn't make sense, but I was willing to try anything. I bought one. I started to walk. I walked to religious music. To Neil Diamond. To songs that went faster and faster.

Slowly and surely my senses became clearer. I was not wavering anymore, and I could stay at the computer for longer periods of time.

One morning, a knock sounded at the door. I answered it and my granddaughter, now two-and-a-half, rushed into my arms as she always does. "Cookies, Ganny?" she asked in her soft, shy voice.

"Oh, Mom, did I tell you I got the interview with the agency?" my daughter, now a social worker, said in that excited, breathless way of hers.

"Outside, outside!" Ariel started to shriek.

"Tell me on our walk, hon," I replied to Ravonna. "I want to hear all about it, but first let's take Ariel to see the river again."

We heard the sound of the geese as they rounded up their families. They appeared to be looking forward to the long flight ahead of them, somewhere that would be warm and sunny when the river would be hard and frozen.

I breathed in its smells, drank in the autumn colors, and felt alive with my granddaughter's hand tightly in mine. She squealed in delight as Ravonna and I swung her between us on the winding, dusty path, taking us nowhere, yet getting us there.

Mirrorstones
by Ann E. Byrnes

I

My journey is to find what was lost from within
I only find mirrorstones all around my skin
I want to see the black and white and the perilous grey (sic)
These stones help me distinguish the hues on the way
All around me are mirrorstones
All this time they've been reflecting me.[7]

A young girl makes her way over the wobbly stile that crosses the barbed-wire fence near the kitchen door of her old stone house. It is a short excursion across the meadow to the creek that cuts through the rolling hills of her rural Maryland home. She has a place here. Her younger brother plays on the other side of the creek where a steep slope rises from the pasture, with a shallow ledge in the middle, like a double-humped camel. She and her six siblings call this "the mountain."

Summer swelters in this part of the state; the girl wears only her white cotton underpants as she wades in the clear cool water. The creek's bottom is soft and sandy in spots, but the water runs mostly over rocks that have tumbled down the hillside. Erosion has broken many into glistening pebbles, which beckon the child like diamonds.

"Let's collect treasure to hide by the gopher hole," her brother calls down from a huge fieldstone embedded in the mountain. "If we bury it deep enough no one will ever find it."

"What about the gopher?" she conjectures.

"Good thinking," the boy agrees. "I'll scout out a good spot. We can mark it with something secret."

Water and sediment drain down her thin legs, past her ankles, as she scoops up waterlogged pebbles in her sun-browned hands. A crayfish, ugly and fierce, scuttles away when his dark hideaway is disturbed. She

---

[7]Chris Noyes, "Mirrorstones"

lets out a little cry of surprise: "Yikes!" For a few moments she stands admiring the glassy, opaque stones in her palms, so full of mystery and promise, like a gypsy's crystal ball.

She knows by the time she climbs up the steep hill to meet her brother, the stones in her hands will be dry, their reflections left behind in the stream's current. Still, she is free to decide on her own treasure, and where to lay it. As the peeper frogs call into the dusk, her main concern, simple and significant, is whether or not she will remember her own hiding spot.

The girl has become a woman, and she has a daughter who wades in the stream with her. Paths remain in the woods from her childhood explorations. Last winter, after a blizzard dropped over three feet of snow, they dug out one of the long paths. Their collection of walking sticks lean against the wall by the front door of the home they have made for themselves.

II

If these walls were breathing,
if these walls could speak,
they'd betray the secrets
of the house on the shaded street.

The handed down tradition
of planting a bitter seed.
A seed that grows in anger,
that blooms in bleak decor.
And hides behind these walls
implanted inside the boy next door.
broken in our own house.
There's a crack in the wall where we live.
Something is getting out.[8]

One day a tall and bearded man, with flashing blue eyes, approaches the woman. He stands on the bank of the streambed, and they talk and laugh and become friends. "I used to like being alone," she says. "Now when I'm alone my heart aches for you." She comes to trust the man, and

---

[8] Greg Greenway, "Crack In The Wall"

when he says he has a strong boat that could carry them all, she believes him. "And both shall row, my love and I."[9] Without hesitation, the woman boards the boat, and they embark down the stream, full throttle. The sparkling pebbles pass below her along with the current, which manipulates the boat.

"Perhaps your concerns are premature," my obstetrician assured me on the telephone when I called for his counsel. "Give it another week or two," he suggested.

But that wasn't necessary. I knew I was pregnant. At age forty-one. Unmarried, unplanned. Richard, the father, un-divorced and, I would soon learn, unstable. Disastrous.

Four days after my call to the doctor, Richard and I planned to meet with my counselor and friend, Gail[10], and then drive to the doctor's office for the official pregnancy test.

"I want to be with you every step of the way, to get through this together," Richard had said. Yet, as we sat across from Gail in her office, the tension between us became as tangible as a concrete wall. The man I loved and trusted, the keen vitality of his spirit and the fire in his clear blue eyes, had retreated behind that wall and unexplainably taken on the dark, lurking disposition of a cornered animal.

I neither knew nor suspected that a crack had cleaved within his psyche. The tinseled veneer of his emotional stability had snapped with the abruptness of a broken fan belt, its frayed ends flapping around its pulleys. Then a band of light broke through the crevice of his sudden transformation, just enough to illuminate a harsh new reality.

We tried to muddle through to some solution, but a clear sense of impasse remained. Without warning, Richard brought the session to a climactic ending: "I have to walk away from you," he said. His face trembled, as did his voice and hands.

I returned his frenzied stare, searching for a hint of the person I thought I knew. A caring, passionate, contemplative, funny man. I saw no trace of him. Gail's brow creased.

"This is the way you're going to tell me?" I cried in disbelief. "In somebody's office? With no explanation? You said you wanted to put things together, not tear them apart."

---

[9] From a traditional folk song.

[10] Not the same Gail as writer of Foreword, Gail E. Parsons, R.N., M.A.

Unable to outlast his demons, the man succumbed, fleeing in defenseless terror to a nearby church, where he wept uncontrollably in the vacant sanctuary.

Gail held me tight as I prepared to leave, tears streaming down both our faces. She grasped my shoulders: "You cannot waste emotional energy on a sick man's chaos. You have other matters to attend to. Above all, you have to take care of yourself."

I drove to the medical plaza in a disoriented haze. Before meeting with the doctor, I ate lunch in the cafeteria. The blue-plate special: cone-head turkey croquettes, mashed potatoes, glutinous gravy, lukewarm corn, and a carton of skim milk. I forced myself to eat, watching the outside world from a box of solitary detachment. I thought of Dr. Seuss' *Horton the Elephant,* hatching his eggs, ambushed in a cage made of jungle branches.

The lab technician drew some blood. The nurse readied me for a sonogram. "The other usual tests can be postponed," the doctor directed. "They won't be necessary should the fetus be aborted."

His handsome features and plastic demeanor reminded me of a Ken doll, come alive. I got dressed, then heard his report. "Unfortunately, the results seem to be positive."

I froze in a purgatory of fear and disorder, but could perceive of no other solution than abortion. I was already raising one child alone, struggling to manage financially while working tirelessly at completing my undergraduate degree. I did not have it in me to bring another child into such tempestuous circumstances.

Although the doctor's usual carefree smile escaped his features, his matter-of-fact approach seemed as sheer as the bandage on the inside of my elbow, and just as effective in thwarting the runoff of the situation.

This was a posh, middle-class practice, comprised of polished physicians. When on call, my doctor breezed through the maze of the office floor plan, dressed in scrubs under his white coat that flowed behind him like a cape. His red high-top sneakers emphasized the unpredictable nature of the female reproductive system.

But on that day, his upbeat and efficient style offered me little comfort. I felt like an oddball, as out of place as a *Mad Magazine* among the glossy covers of the prenatal publications adorning the crowded waiting room.

Due to my "advanced maternal age," we discussed genetic testing, in case I chose to place the baby for adoption. He scrawled on a prescription slip the name of an abortion clinic, a town outside of Baltimore, a telephone number.

"Give them a call," he said in the same tone in which he may have advised me to try a vinegar douche. "But you'll need to wait until ten to twelve weeks gestation. Otherwise the fetus won't be large enough to ensure complete removal of all the growth cells. Give it some thought, talk to people you know. Consider your options. You have some time."

He scribbled *10-12 wks* on the note before zipping the page off the pad and moving on to his next patient.

Back home, the song of peepers taunted me as I sat behind the wheel of my car, staring blankly at the wooded valley below my home where I lived with my seven-year-old daughter, April. "We remember where those treasures are stored," the invisible frogs intoned. Several minutes passed before I realized I had not turned off the ignition.

I turned the key in my four-room-apartment door. The damp breeze suffocated me. I realized what the peepers were telling me: I couldn't remember the path to my hidden gemstones.

I crossed the threshold into the loneliest place I had ever known, an eclipsing labyrinth of disconnected corridors. Now, instead of being the steadfast single mother of a bright, well-adjusted first grader, I was confused and forced to consider forestalling my education, again.

I no longer had Richard to rely on as best friend, confidant, lover. I had overlooked the signs. The white-hot glow of our relationship had overshadowed the countless instances of no substance, no progress between us.

I had dismissed his unreliability, distraction, and emotional detachment. He often said, "I want to build a house for us with my own two hands." But this, along with every other goal we set, was not backed up with action, never managing to come to fruition. It became painfully obvious that Richard remained decidedly on the fringes of my life.

The following weeks passed at glacial speed, while I waited for the life within me to grow large enough to abort. I attended classes, groped through endless assignments in biology, engineering, animal science, literature, and research methods. I helped April with her homework, shuttled her to gymnastics and swimming lessons, exercised, shopped for groceries, paid bills—everyday activities all shrouded in anguish. The telephone screamed with silence.

One morning I called the number the doctor had given me. "When can you come in?" the receptionist asked. "We could see you tomorrow at noon."

I explained that I was only six seeks pregnant. "Oh, well, do you want to set something up for next month? Otherwise, we only need twenty-four hours notice."

I suppose she was trying to minimize the impact, but I was disturbed by the casual approach to "the procedure."

Somewhere deep within my solitary confinement was the itch, perhaps, of a baby beseeching its own life. So I scheduled my next prenatal appointment with the staff nurse-midwife. She genuinely tried to understand and help me. Although another nurse interrupted us several times, we spent over an hour discussing the complexities of adoption.

I left with a handful of information about agencies and legalities. I wrote several piercing letters to people I thought might be interested in adoption: *Dear Cindy and Joe, Let me come straight to the point…*

I conferred with my sister, who has two adopted children and is active in adoption counseling. "First of all," she replied, "I would never advise anyone to have an abortion. I just think it's wrong."

I made an appointment with an adoption counselor. She sat beside me in my small living room, listening as I recounted my circumstances. "How will I explain to April that her baby brother or sister will be given away?" I agonized.

She held my hand. "Give yourself some time, to put some of the pieces together. I would, however, recommend you have the genetic tests done. The sooner the better. You have time," she repeated the doctor's words. "These things have a way of working themselves out."

The next week I went to the hospital for the genetic test and a sonogram. The moment I saw the color photograph of the shrimp-like being with a sweet little face growing inside me, I knew termination was out of the question.

When the counselor from the adoption agency called several weeks later, I was close to making my decision. Then on a Saturday, Richard appeared on my doorstep. He had been in counseling and seemed to be back on his feet. His passionate blue eyes shone clear above his beard. He had brought an aloe plant as a symbol, he said, of re-growth.

"I am committed to you, to us, to our family," he promised. "And I want to keep the baby."

I was cautious about this turnaround, but it appeared to be genuine and offered me a solution. We waited for the genetic test results while sifting through baby name books. We renewed our plans to rent a house before the school year resumed. Richard spoke of marriage, once his divorce became finalized.

The genetic test came back indicating that if the baby was a girl, she would have Turner's Syndrome[11], but not if a boy. Richard and April went with me for a follow-up sonogram. The technician typed *Hi Mom and Dad* on the film, along with the letter *p* and an arrow pointing to a tiny penis. We decided to name the baby Noah.

Richard signed a lease on a house. We shopped for a simple wedding dress. And I continued studying part-time at the community college. At last, it seemed our dream of being a family had become a reality.

Although something didn't feel quite right, I attributed this to both moving and living with someone after many years of being on my own. I dismissed Richard's disjointed memory, his "forgetting" to follow through on simple matters, not retaining important conversations.

"I'll take care of sending the rent check," he would say. But it took several days for him to write the check, which would then sit, stalled, in his van for more days, until the payment was late. When I asked him about it, he put me off or made excuses as weak and viscous as pale molasses.

When I questioned these tactics, he replied, "I'll get it done on my timetable, not yours."

One Wednesday in October, Richard said he had an appointment in Washington, D.C., to discuss a potential assignment. I stayed behind working in the office of his commercial photography studio. He drove my car because it got better gas mileage.

Other than expressing annoyance that he had borrowed all of my cash and returned without any, my car a quart low on oil, and an empty gas tank, I let the incident pass.

The next week, however, a package arrived while Richard was out. Inside it were not the usual photo proofs or film orders I had expected. Instead, it contained a book, two CDs, and a two-page handwritten letter.

My hands trembled. I had given Richard the CDs and book almost a year ago. I read the letter three times. *Thank you for last Wednesday,* the woman wrote in neat, pretty script.

---

[11] A disorder resulting in stunted stature, reduced mental capacity, and varying degrees of ambiguous genitalia.

I paced the studio. The lyrics of an old song ticker-taped across my intellect: "A question's not really a question, if you know the answer too."[12]

It took several minutes for the receptionist to bring Richard to the telephone. "What's the matter?" he asked. "What's going on?"

"You tell me." I told him about the package.

"Oh yes, I told you about that meeting."

A lie. Blatant, uncharacteristic. The first of many that would pile up like amassing kidney stones.

Richard arrived home late that night. He found a dark house—I had turned off the porch light.

"I've been living a lie for months," he confessed. "Right after your call, I called her and told her she had ruined my life."

"She didn't ruin your life. You did. And there are others involved besides just you."

He explained the relationship as an "Internet thing" that became a *Fatal Attraction.* The twenty-two-year old had threatened to harass his sons, who lived with his ex-wife.

"What kind of a person are you?" I cried. "How could you do this to me, to your children, to yourself?"

"I don't know. It was just a casual thing. I fell apart. It was a compulsion. It didn't mean anything. I just did it."

I insisted that he leave.

That wild look—the rabid eyes, the frantic movements as he grabbed some clothes—sprang up once more, as it had months ago in Gail's office. "I'm not insane!" he screamed. "I may be sick, but I'm not crazy." He stormed out of the house, leaving me standing in the shadows of the kitchen, its walls reverberating with hysteria.

III

> *For all the dark passages that make it hard to see*
> *for all the dirt you gotta dig to set yourself free*
> *for all the reasons peace don't come easily*
> *There's a real fine line this side of sanity.*[13]

---

[12] John Prine, "Far From Me"

[13] Dee Carstensen and Mike Nainieri, "Hemingway's Shotgun"

The snug little boat, which carried the woman and her love, diverged from the river's gentle current to a tributary of dangerous rapids. In one vital instant, the whitewater swept away the boat's oars. The man screamed that he was jumping overboard. The woman gripped the sides of the boat, white-knuckled, gasping for breath. The wet, polished pebbles tumbled, without leeway, under the boat's erratic passage.

I found myself dealing with a man who recoiled headlong from his irresponsible behavior into the great escape of suicide. He had considered it at least once before, when his marriage broke up. Somewhere there was a cinderblock, a rope, a specified creek of the Chesapeake Bay, where he had planned to sink himself.

He spent the night I kicked him out at the foot of the Chesapeake Bay Bridge, thinking about jumping from the highest span into the murky water below.

The bridge patrol took him to an emergency room. He assured the staff that he would contact his therapist the next day, so they released him. At first, he slept in the back of his van, parked in a church parking lot, showering each morning at the YMCA. When the weather turned colder, he slept on a cot at his studio.

Two days after he left, I dialed the number on the package from the other woman. "This is Ann Byrnes," I said. "Richard's fiancée." I asked her about their relationship, if she had made any threats, if she knew about me.

"No," she answered. "For months now, Richard has been telling me how much he cares for me." She had made no threats, and knew nothing about April or the pregnancy. "It's all in the letters he wrote." She had saved them. I asked for copies.

When confronted, Richard confirmed that theirs had been a relationship fueled by his own affectations, expressed in countless e-mail letters, many phone calls, and the exchanging of music. "I thought I told her about the pregnancy," he said vaguely. "I was sure we had discussed the abortion issue."

"Doesn't seem like something that would slip your mind," I replied. "And what about our engagement? Was that another detail that wasn't worth mentioning? If you want to do the disappearing act with yourself, that's one thing, but you're not going to conveniently erase me."

109

"It wasn't like that," he replied feebly. "I never stopped loving you, at the core of who I am. Believe me. I was out of control. It had nothing to do with you."

I told him that the letters were being forwarded: "You can do your best to avoid it, but the truth will soon be out."

"Let it fly," he said in a fragile tone that did not match the boldness of his words.

Not even my worst suspicions prepared me for what the two bulging parcels of letters contained. Page after page of meticulously composed correspondence, a manipulated seduction wrapped in furtive fantasy. The words matched exactly those spoken to me in the past. A template of courtship. Lies and innuendoes overlapped, snowballing. Fabrications about a glamorous life, a thriving career, a romantic dwelling.

The barbs from the bundles of letters sharpened as I compared them with my calendar: before and after the meeting in Gail's office, on the day of my amniocentesis, the day after we moved, minutes after I left the studio one night to go home and prepare dinner for the family, and on my birthday.

The worst were the cassette tapes he had made for her, compilations of songs that had been special between us, many from albums I had given him as gifts. My gut wrenched as the familiar voices turned from art to poison. Here was The Indigo Girls singing "The Power of Two." David Wilcox: "I got a weakness for strong chemistry." Sarah McLachlan: "My love, you know that you're my best friend. Let nothing come between us." Bonnie Raitt: "In matters of the heart, there is nothing a fool won't get used to." Defiled verse.

"Is nothing sacred?" I railed. These were fugues of madness. But Richard didn't remember selecting the songs and could not coherently address the making of the tapes.

These were the darkest days of his breakdown. We were frightfully lost without a map. The man I had known had withdrawn into the raisin of a once plump, succulent grape. My heart was shattered. Like a wayward navigator on the open seas, I realized that I had been alone all along.

IV

And the ice talks to the river
And the geese talk to themselves
Will they fly all night if there's no place to land?
A place to land is open water
And open water he can't use
When it's hard enough to find a place to stand
When the ice gives in beneath you
You know, it changes how you dream
And you will never be the same again.[14]

The turbulent waters threatened to capsize the small boat. The man beseeched his companion to take hold of his hand. But she saw, then, that his shining white armor, besides being handsome and slick, was heavy. Through the turbulent flow of the jagged ride, she instinctively knew that if she took his hand they would both sink to the stony bottom, drowned under the weight of the cumbrous veneer.

My life took on a third-person dimension, as if I was narrating my own story. I was a broken shell of my former self. Deadlocked and directionless once more, the assembly line of my daily duties passing mechanically. Desperately trying to maintain my crumbling concentration, I somehow kept up with my schoolwork, and managed to get "A's" in both my classes. I spent hours laboring over statistics and earth science homework, studying the earth's core, the focus of earthquakes, the means of huge probabilities.

Yet my own center was a slipped fault line. During my six-month checkup, sitting across from a new doctor I had never seen before, I broke down in tears. At night, I would lie alone in bed, wailing at the stone-silent plaster walls: "What am I doing here?" The house that had once been so full of hope now felt like a tomb. I wanted to leave it all behind and run away, but I knew that a stable home was important for my children and me.

---

[14]John Gorka, "Temporary Road"

Thus began a solitary journey of searching for myself amid the rubble of a demolished dream. Somewhere, mirrored in the dark stones of this unforeseen tragedy, was the secret that the peepers remembered. Somewhere under the debris remained a fragment of erosion's glistening pebbles.

My relationship with Richard was reduced to wrought-up telephone conversations, dominated by his dark depression and volatility. We were chasing our own tails in a cycle of his feelings of guilt, shame, and failure, and my deep hurt and anger.

Through drug and psychiatric therapy, a mother lode, having lain latent for most of Richard's life, began to be extracted. It was a dangerous shaft, marked by firedamp explosions and tailings.

His rendition of a pleasant childhood had been the product of repressed incidences of extreme neglect and sexual abuse. Offenses were uncovered bit by bit: his father's abandonment, an absentee mother, and poverty.

At the age of nine, there were innumerable occurrences of emotional and physical coercion by a homosexual male couple named Frank and Doc. The next year, separate brutal assaults and a rape by a licentious drifter, known in the neighborhood only as "Wolf."

Unjustly, the young Richard trusted no one with his shameful secrets. No one acknowledged his shaken composure. He had revealed nothing, keeping the terror of it at bay by stashing the malignancy in a subconscious vault.

The boy had built his own fortress, depending on the safe box of avoidance rather than the security provided by those who should have protected him. He spent hours on the top bunk, eyes boring desperate fantasies of escape into the blank ceiling.

I accompanied Richard to counseling sessions, where I sat round-bellied and squarely incensed. There, the dark dichotomies of our failing relationship began a new cycle. I was outraged and sympathetic about his cruel past, and indignant that the perversions had victimized him, but reverberated down to those tangled in the web of the damaged adult-child. However, the wounds I had suffered prevented me from being able to fully comfort and support him.

One of the topics in these sessions was "resolution by discovery," whereby I wound up holding Richard's "lapels" and getting "in the face" of his behavior, rather than his being accountable for it himself. He desperately wanted to be responsible for his own lapels, but, like so many times in the past, he was unable to repair the short circuit between his words and desires, and his actions.

These sessions added to my sense of disconnection. I was often frustrated by the therapist's guarded, reactive approach to getting too involved in my portion of the circumstances. I was welcome to attend with Richard, but he was the patient. I played an auxiliary role. Distinct boundaries were established, over which I was not permitted to cross.

"You've been seeing your therapist for months," I would say outside of the meetings. "I know you're comfortable working with her, but what progress is being made?"

Neither one of us knew enough at the time to pursue treatment by a professional who was experienced in issues of childhood sexual abuse. It didn't occur to me to insist that the situation be addressed in a holistic manner, that there were children involved, that the family members also needed help in dealing with these abnormalities. And I didn't notice that the therapist had not made Richard accountable for his lack of honesty and commitment to their relationship. He had, of course, deceived her as well.

On our erratic road together, the one thing remaining constant was Richard's impassioned declarations that, regardless of the opposing actions spawned by his sickness, he clearly loved me and wanted to get back to being himself so that we could have a normal, healthy life together. Yet we were stalled in volatility. The harmony of our lives had been replaced with a torque of hurtful disagreement.

Though only eight years old, April knew that things were very different from the stability she had known for most of her life. On December 17, she wrote on a slip of Santa-faced notepaper: *Dear Santa, Can you send Richard out of me and my mom's life or please make him be better to my mom and me. Love, April.*

A few weeks later, due to the sudden complications of preeclampsia, it was decided that Noah would be delivered three weeks early. As the nurse started the labor-inducing I.V., I quipped, "Let the games begin."

After a rapid and intense labor, the tiny, five-pound body emerged from the birth canal. "It's a peanut!" the doctor exclaimed. The tiny boy's eyes flickered with his father's azure and his mother's curiosity.

At two days old, Noah's weight dipped below five pounds and he was diagnosed with failure-to-thrive. He and I spent most of his first two weeks in the hospital. Once we returned home, I was instructed to adhere to a strict feeding schedule. This, added to a raging case of infant colic, sapped my dwindling strength and confidence.

113

Overloaded, my systems began to fail. Just as Noah began to sleep through the night, I developed insomnia. Paradoxically, the more exhausted I became, the more difficult it was to sleep. Calls to my doctor offered little help.

After several weeks, the situation deteriorated quickly. Within a few days, I went from waking up early in the morning to getting only two or three hours of restless sleep at night. Just functioning was difficult; I dreaded the start of each day, and feared the sleepless nights.

"Dear God, you've given me the gift of this baby, please show me how to handle this." I was desperate, and on the verge of collapse.

Finally, Richard insisted that I go to the emergency room. The stressors of emotional upheaval, a difficult pregnancy, sleep deprivation, hormonal changes, a reaction to an injection of Depo Provara (a contraceptive), and adjusting to life with a demanding newborn, had depleted my coping abilities. I had a "full-blown case" of postpartum depression.

"I feel like I should be able to handle this better," I said to the social worker at the hospital's clinic.

"Oh, so you have high standards," she replied with a little knowing smile. "You're feeling exactly the way you should be feeling."

The weeks that followed focused on frantic experimentation to find an effective type and dosage of medication. Treatment was further complicated by my commitment to breast-feeding, which limited the choice of drugs I could safely take. I had always had confidence in my parenting instincts, yet now I felt completely inadequate as a mother, and utterly pessimistic that my life would ever be put back together again. Months passed before I moved from teetering on the brink to safety.

One day in the spring I stumbled across several letters and a poem hidden away on Richard's office computer. The poem, "Remembrance," spoke of placing past love in a box for safekeeping. When confronted, Richard admitted that this was a very recent correspondence from a high school girlfriend, a repeat of his behavior of the past. Once more, he had not told me, nor his therapist.

A heated street-side argument ensued in front of the studio. "Stay away from me and my children," I screamed, throwing cassette tapes at him.

"You're overreacting," he implored. But by now I recognized this as a minimizing tactic. My gut feeling told me that my response was justified.

As I drove away I was struck by the fact that, presumably having grown accustomed to these arguments, Noah had fallen asleep in the back seat.

Late that night I received a phone call from Richard's therapist saying he had been taken by ambulance to the psychiatric unit of the hospital in Cambridge. That was the last official contact we had with that therapist. She did not visit or even telephone Richard.

As Richard's five-day hospital stay progressed, more pieces of the puzzle were revealed. We had a long meeting with the doctors, who explained their suspicion that Richard had been depressed for most of his life, severely so in recent years. When his pattern of avoidance caused him to neglect grieving his failed marriage and separation from his two older sons, it triggered post-traumatic stress syndrome and uncovered events and emotions from the past that had been repressed for decades.

This was the first straightforward diagnosis we had received. "It's a contagious disease," the head doctor explained. "Its mechanism wants to counteract any positive productivity of its victims, insidiously working toward ultimate destruction. This would account for Richard's systematic dismantling of anything that moves toward progression." Further, they confirmed that Richard's treatment over the previous two years should have been much more aggressive and preventative.

On Father's Day, Noah and I were admitted through the locked security door of the psychiatric ward for a visit. A scattering of smiling, yet somehow off-center patients ogled over the tiny five-month-old infant as we made our way to the patient lounge area. I felt uncomfortable and unsure of my own motivations for being there.

The contradictions of our relationship had intensified: I was angry with Richard for his recurring dishonesty, yet how could I turn my back on him at a time like this? The visit was short and painful, another staging of the impasse of derangement that our lives had become.

Richard was discharged and assigned to a new therapist. He was raw and on the edge. His unpredictable tirades were frightening. I was determined to remain in the background of his treatment, to let him take full responsibility. Yet, when he became increasingly unstable, I called his new therapist. Immediately I recognized the cool, guarded economy of words and emotion: "Thank you for letting me know. I can't always monitor just how my clients are doing outside of my office."

The following day she admitted Richard to the hospital's day program. I felt reassured by his receiving more intensive treatment, but was uneasy about the fact that his therapist hadn't detected the severity of his instability. She simply advised me to "let the professionals handle it" and gave Richard the number of a crisis hot line, where he sought comfort from anonymous voices across long-distance wires.

The patterns persisted, seemingly unshaken. The suicidal tendencies continued. Forgiveness, compassion, nurturing, outrage, setting limits—it seemed that nothing could interrupt the turning cogs. Regardless of his determination, Richard's fears and fortifications would not come down by will; the process was tediously incremental. The old blues songs urge the afflicted to "quit your lowdown ways." In practice, reform was far more complicated and erratic.

Whenever a breakthrough seemed close, broken promises, mistrust, and undisclosed factors would appear from all corners of Richard's life: misplaced priorities, hidden events, relations, debts. Life would settle down, run on an even keel for hours, days, weeks. Then, like a wild roller coaster ride, the hurtful, scatting dualism would reappear.

A crucial period began one Sunday afternoon when my landlady called to say she was putting the house up for sale and terminating my lease. She had never been understanding about my circumstances. Decent housing was scarce, especially for an unemployed single mother. I was terrified that we would be squeezed out with no place to live.

"So there you have it," I told myself. "The reality is you're on your own, with nobody to count on but yourself, and maybe God." I had to ask myself some hard questions: "At what point does devotion become unhealthy? Is there a vertex where rising above leads to dragging down?"

A year had passed with plenty of action but little headway. In August, I wrote in my journal:

> *Life is a mess of confusion, pain and uncertainty. I am on my own again. What do I have to hold on to? I never, ever thought it would turn out like this. I don't have a family, and I don't have my independence. Again, I am faced with building a life of my own. I've done it before, I can do it again. The way will open. It's not up to me to rescue Richard; it's up to me to protect my family. It's myself I'm going to give the chances to now.*

V

Do I know this woman
She was always waiting
In the shadows of my room
I turn my head and she's standing in my place
I hear her voice getting stronger by the day
Is that my hair? – Are those my eyes?
The mirror never lies
So who's that woman staring in my face?
Do I know this woman
She has left behind the fears
That haunted in her past
That's my hair
Those are my eyes
Now I'm that woman. [15]

I knew this would be a long, lonely pilgrimage. But I refused to run on empty, stalled at the Last Chance Texaco. [16] Trust, healing, identity had to come from within. I would have to rely not on my lover, or my family, or the professionals, but on the light and strength inside of me.

One afternoon I received a call from Richard: "The clinic just called to say that my appointment has to be cancelled because my therapist has resigned. Just disappeared, with no explanation whatsoever to her patients. I thought she was supposed to be helping me work through my feeling of abandonment, and now she's abandoned me herself."

"I knew it!" I exclaimed. "I knew that woman couldn't be trusted. Next time I won't be intimidated by these so-called professionals."

I wrote a letter to the director of the behavior health program outlining the negative impact this type of attitude has on the family of the patient. There was no reply.

Richard interviewed several private doctors in town and selected his next therapist himself. Using a direct and proactive approach, it was quickly determined that much of his abusive behavior resulted from unexpressed rage, much of which was misdirected.

---

[15] Susan Graham White, "Who's That Woman"
[16] Rickie Lee Jones, "Last Chance Texaco"

I was the one who realized that his anger at his mother for putting her education before the needs of her children was being enacted through Richard's hostility toward my schooling.

"Sure," Richard's doctor confirmed, as if it was plain as day, "it's misplaced anger."

One day Richard fervently proclaimed that he was behind me all the way in my endeavors and wanted to know all about my studies. He asked for the telephone number of the voice mail system being used by my language class, so he could call and listen to an assignment on which I had been praised by the professor. Days later, when I called to check my messages, there was a notification that the assignment had not been accessed for over ten days, and had been automatically erased.

"What happened to calling about my class work?" I asked.

"I lost the number," he replied. "I was afraid to tell you."

I knew I had had enough. Like the proverbial straw that broke the camel's back, I knew the equilibrium had shifted.

"I'm not your mother," I stated. "I'm not your father, or Frank or Doc, or Wolf. I will not stand in for them in the boxing ring of your anger. I will not have them living with me. I'm going to move on and make a better life."

I saw that I could not control Richard's behavior or change his past. But there were things I could do. I could refuse to become another parasitic victim of the abuse and neglect. I could nurture my own family, and keep it strong and intact. I could raise my son to be an honest man. I could pursue my education and my writing career. These were underpinnings I *could* protect against deterioration.

I could try to understand Richard's struggles, but I would not commit to a life of cyclical incongruity. My own needs would no longer be neglected. After almost two years of battling, I told Richard, "I'm taking back my heart," but it echoed, "I still believe,"[17] like a ticking metronome heedless of its surroundings.

I looked in the mirror and saw the eyes of that little girl wading in the creek in her white cotton underpants. The essence of who she was, and who I am, had not been destroyed in the ruins. I could trust and value that; it would not fail me. It had been there all along, a stronghold more akin to the properties of light than stone, that could withstand the forces of decay, and remain standing.

---

[17] Susan Warner, "I Still Believe"

Like a flash of lightening in the summer sky, the woman in the boat remembers the pebbles that once sparkled in her own small hands. "They're still there, right where I stashed them," she thinks. "I can find them again."

The sound of the peepers can be faintly heard over the dissonance of the rapids. "There is another choice," she realizes. "I don't have to stay in this foundering vessel. Nor do I have to be taken down into the depths of the raging water.

"There's nothing to be gained by trying to save the boat, or going down with it. I can make my way back to solid ground, where I can stand firm, where the sun shines warm and comforts my face, and dances on the possibilities held in the mirrorstones."

She begins to maneuver the little oarless boat through the cascading water. The rushing current resists her strokes of determination. Her solitary efforts may seem futile and foolish amid the river's panorama. Still, she is free to decide on her own treasure, and to lay it up where she might.

Tying Slipknots
by Debbie Tomasovic

My tense knuckles glow white. Tightly clutching the steering wheel, I keep one eye on the road and one ear on the vibrations emanating from my rooftop. "I can do this, I can do this," becomes my mantra, as I curse another traffic light for beaming red. While stewing at the light, I come to the satisfying conclusion that 1999 has unfolded as my year of courage, and my newest adventure must surely fill the bill.

My independent friend, Rita, assured me that my self-confidence would beautifully blossom the first time I kayaked alone. So, here I sit, in busy downtown traffic, accompanied by a trustworthy lifejacket and what must look like an enormous plastic yellow banana strapped to the roof of my little gray Honda.

As I endure the ridiculously long light, I think back to the first time I observed Rita's technique of loading the kayak onto her car, by herself. I learned so much that day: weight distribution, the use of fulcrums, even how to tie slipknots. All this for a woman who occasionally berated herself for misperceived clumsiness and pitifully poor coordination. Who knows? By the time I return the kayak, along with my outpouring of appreciation, I may wield it about with the same confident abandon.

I marveled, as I drove away from the kayak exchange, at the wonderful risks I was taking this year. My meandering journey to this endeavor started four years ago when I moved into my lakeside apartment, alone. That first separation from my best friend and roommate produced both fear and growth. I was on my own, for the first time. Meals alone, paying bills alone, grocery shopping alone. None of this sounded the least bit appealing to a woman who had not been able to tolerate more than two hours in her bedroom before peeking her head out to see what her roommate was up to.

So who knew I would fall in love with living alone? The freedom to blast Aretha Franklin late into the night, to leap up from my writing table to dance erratically to a driving beat, to accept phone calls at all hours, to sit and marvel at my wondrous abode without interruption. I have discovered the unadulterated joy of ordering pizza without negotiating the toppings, of attending outdoor concerts and leaving when I am good and ready, and of making unscheduled treks to the ice cream shop or bookstore for a quick fix, without justification.

Of course, this wondrous perspective didn't suddenly sprout from the tender soil overnight. I spend many a night pining for companionship, for accompaniment, for something rocky road cannot always satisfy. I sometimes struggle, grappling for a firm grip on the slippery, ever evasive lesson of self-nurturing. Such empty moments call for the same reassuring assessment required to miraculously mount a kayak "too heavy to lift" onto my car, with nothing but my own two hands.

Often, when I stand before my mirror, wondering what is to become of me, I look long and deep into my pale, blue eyes and invite myself out to play. To weave my mountain bike between trees and stumps. To dip my big toe into the Gulf waters, mid-November. To flip on the radio, promising to break into song, regardless of the tune. I drift endlessly from searching to discovering and back again, knowing this none-too-tidy process will repeat itself. My penchant for discovery will always resurface. All she requires is my allowing her room to breathe. To be. I am learning…

Rolling down my window, I feel the breeze and sun on my browning skin. Feeling quite strong and energized, I observe other drivers observing me. I imagine their thoughts regarding this confident woman, driving around town alone, with a kayak on her roof. I sit taller in the seat, just imagining their admiration! Just as likely, the other hostages of this traffic entrapment mask their curious concern for the brunette with the banana strapped to her car, doing a far too dramatic rendition of "Hot Child in the City" while awaiting her chance to turn.

I drift to the first time I kayaked. The sun and breeze accompanied me that day, too. Pushing from shore, I rocked and tipped while trying to find my balance. When I found my rhythm, I pulled myself through the water with eager curiosity. I made my way to the mouth of the bay, passing roosting pelicans on the left and fishing herons on the right. The water mesmerized me as the sun touched its surface with brilliant reflection. I coasted for a moment to give thanks. Thanks to Mother Earth for all her beauty, thanks to good friends who entrust me with cherished possessions such as kayaks, and thanks to myself for the courage to explore this new place, to be alone with nature.

Suddenly full of zest, I pulled hard through the rough waters. I loved riding out the waves, negotiating the currents, and passing sailboats. The wind whipped hard, invigorating me, feeding me. The larger the white caps, the more alive I felt. So intimate with the water, kissed by the sun, revitalized by the wind, I felt utterly one with it all, as if in a moving meditation. A chilly wave splashed over me, as the water kindly requested that I keep my singing to a reasonable volume. I smiled and laughed out loud.

Once again, as I heft the Kayak off the car and over to the shoreline, I offer thanks for the lavish freedom I have to laugh out loud while reading in my peach-colored chair, to call a friend for companionship during a disturbing movie, to smile and nod "hello" to attractive strangers. Moments that scare me, exhilarate me, and relax me. They all seem necessary, the calm and the breakers, both on the water and off.

Today, in the water, I set my sights on a random target in the distance and launch myself towards it. I glide to a stop in the center of the bay and lay my oar aside. Peace and quiet envelop me as a sailboat approaches. The bearded, leathery captain pulls alongside my vessel to inquire about the kayak's maneuverability. Full of pride, I announce, "It's very easy." He sails on, leaving me to ebb and flow with the constant current. To paddle on or float freely, I have the choice. What complete contentment.

As I cut through the water, I think about the last few months and all I have accomplished. So many firsts, like deciding to enjoy a piece of my vacation on the water alone, not because I am alone, but because I want to be alone. Charged by this thought, I pull harder and deeper with my oar. In front of me, egrets sail a few feet above the water. Fish leap into the air to clean their gills. A dolphin cruises by, peeking above the surface to investigate this yellow boat's inhabitant.

A Native American saying suggests that we are never alone, because the land, the sky, the trees and animals always accompany us.

Occasionally, I satisfy my hunger for companionship simply by digesting nature... I am instantly distracted by a driving need to fish about for the one remaining, crushed granola bar left abandoned in the bottom of my backpack.

Back on shore, strapping the borrowed kayak to my car, I ponder the rest of my vacation's itinerary. To do something, to do nothing. To dine out or eat leftover Chinese food. To rent a movie with friends or stay up late into the night, watching a *Wonder Woman* rerun with girlish admiration.

As my mother and I strolled through the woods earlier this month, she relayed the contents of a brief chat she had had with another teacher:

"They'll never make me a grandpa!" He bitterly declared.

"A grandpa?"

"Yeah, my two grown kids seem determined to deny me my right to have grandchildren, whom I would gladly spoil beyond recognition."

I imagined my mother nodding silently, with her ever-concerned look, causing her brow to furrow and lips to purse.

"Could you imagine how pressured his kids feel, like if they don't have children, they will utterly disappoint the man who gave them life itself?" she said to me.

A warm wave of relief washed over me. We paused to watch a woodpecker burrow into a sandy palm tree's trunk, in search of a tasty snack.

In time, we turned from his gentle drumming to crunch on through the fallen leaves, our bodies in sync. I marveled at this woman who strode contentedly by my side. Her blue eyes mirror mine, yet hers pierce deeper. We possess similar, slender fingers, except hers are topped with a maroon splash of color, like icing on a cake.

I rediscovered my "larger than life" mother that day, who actually stands two inches shorter than her towering daughter. Distinctly different, yet surprisingly similar. From the moment of my birth, when I began to drink in the world around me, my mother always encouraged me to taste the endless array of sounds, flavors, and colors that textured my world. To play. To ponder, to ask "what if?"

As we meandered through the woods, my mother pondered what form her life would have taken if she had entered adulthood during these times. Would she marry or remain single, birth children or remain childfree? I could have insecurely surmised that she regretted giving birth to my brother and me. Instead, I realized that times had changed, and am grateful that I have had options, and a mother who has accepted my choices.

We walked on, listening to the crisp brown leaves beneath our feet, silently contemplating the curious twists and turns our lives had taken. I made a mental note to revisit this wondrous place if I ever get lost in self-pity again. As I often do. There will be another moment of nagging doubt that sneaks up from behind and taps me gingerly on the shoulder. How likely am I to turn once again, staring blankly into that foreboding mirror? Oh, you again... Blank eyes. Searching eyes. Searching for warm reassurance.

Then I will yearn, once again, to embrace my own capacities for creativity, adventure, and the true pleasure found first within before moving outward. To rediscover those marvelous truths that grow forth from knowing who I am. A single, powerful, capable woman who can write with color, dance with vigor, and launch my own kayak into the great, wide world...

With a satisfying sigh, I now turn the corner, onto my own street. My contented eyes fall upon my home, peeking from behind two towering pine trees. As I pull up to my peaceful lakeside apartment, I give thanks for this rich opportunity to live freely, walk lightly, and tie a slipknot, if need be.

The Video
by Dianne Lorang

This story was written many years ago, in response to a friend's journey into widowhood and single parenthood. It is still the best expression I can conjure up of that time, and although it is different from the other stories in this book, because the focus is not on the single woman herself, it demonstrates the immense difficulties some women go through, and how well they do on their own...

It was in color, but it seemed more like black and white, or at the most, a bad colorized version of an old movie. I hadn't been prepared for it that day, the first day I babysat Julie by herself. I usually had her brother Joey, too, but he had started kindergarten. So when Julie was scared to be left at my house without him, her mom, Lisa, had promised her she could watch the video.

I didn't know what it was. "One of Julie's favorites," Lisa had said. So I popped it in and Julie climbed on the couch with her pink blanket and doggie. She hadn't looked at me yet, and shook her head "no" when I asked if she wanted her coat off. I decided to leave her alone for a while, to let her warm up to me. I could still keep an eye on her from the kitchen and the laundry room.

Trouble was, I could also keep an eye on the video. And I could hear it, including her father's voice, which I hadn't heard since he had gone into the hospital in May. Now it was September, and we all knew he wasn't coming home, ever again. At first, he'd been diagnosed as clinically depressed, but nothing had helped. Not even three months of shock treatments.

We'd suspected all along that it had to be something else. Even he hadn't believed the doctors. But there had been no other explanation, until late summer when the exams showed changes, changes that only an irreversible neurological disease can cause. "Six months to a year, maybe even two years," the doctors told Lisa. And she had told her four children.

I hardly ever babysat the two older ones. Jamie was in first grade, and Jen attended second grade when she wasn't in special classes. She used to be the star of this particular video, her first Christmas, until now when

127

Julie was watching it to see her daddy. The daddy she would only remember because of such modern miracles as video camcorders.

Her brother Joey would have his own memories. His father had taken him to the Final Four basketball tournament every year since he was two, even this last year when he drove his old brown Toyota pickup over the Colorado mountains to Salt Lake City, and we all prayed they'd be okay.

Fortunately, when he did get in a minor car wreck the next week, he was on a business trip where people knew him. They contacted company employees who met his return flight to Denver.

The company then forced him to see a doctor, and then another doctor, and then have tests, and finally to take disability. So began his lonely descent into sleepless nights and MTV. If he did fall asleep, it would be on the couch, leaving his wife alone in their king-size bed.

Toward the end, he wouldn't have any trouble sleeping—he slept most of the time. But in the beginning, he was in too much pain. He had trouble explaining it. "My face hurts," he would say. And I remembered back in November that he was having sinus trouble. "It's the polluted air," I told him. "You'll get used to it after a while."

But he never did. His physical symptoms just got worse over the winter. Everyone had noticed his robotic-type movements, then the change in his work, in his reports, in his speech, in the amount of hours he'd have to spend at the office and still get nothing done. He had probably known something was wrong for a long time. Still, when my husband asked him if he was okay, he answered, "I just have a lot on my mind."

He did have worries. A recent move from rural Montana to a suburb of Denver. A larger mortgage. A new position. And a developmentally disabled daughter who was getting worse, not better, as they had hoped with the resources supposedly available in the big city. The same resources that couldn't help him in the end.

The bright geologist who had been valedictorian of both his high school and college classes. The man who had gone on to receive a masters degree and just before his illness, The Young Scientist of the Year Award. I had expected him to be my husband's boss someday, although my husband had once been his.

But in the video, he was healthy again. Cheerful, joking with his brother, singing Christmas carols while his sister played the guitar, tickling his mother, swinging Jen up above him like fathers do. Smiling at Lisa, who had been his high school sweetheart.

I hadn't known him back then, but I could feel his presence in my house now. His youngest child had yet to move from her corner of the couch. I wanted to turn off the VCR, switch to cartoons.

"Julie," I asked, "Do you want to play Legos?" No answer. It had been an hour and the tape was still going.

I wished the wind wasn't blowing. They had predicted snow for that afternoon, and for once, they might be right. I wanted to get out of the house, go for a walk to the park. Julie and Joey had always liked the park.

The tape suddenly went fuzzy. "Good," I thought, "it's over." Julie squirmed for a minute, grabbing at her zipper. I walked over, sat down next to her, and took off her coat. She crawled onto my lap and faced the TV. The video had continued. It was now New Year's Eve.

The warmth of Julie's body seemed to take the chill out of that rare cold autumn day. I wrapped my arms around her and watched her parents and aunt and uncle circling the room in silence. The then-baby Jen was asleep and they were pantomiming their celebration, so as not to wake her.

They might have been singing "Auld Lang Syne," *for old acquaintance be forgot and never brought to mind...*or just reciting good wishes for a "Happy New Year." I couldn't read their lips. No more than I could read this little girl's mind.

I could only imagine what she was thinking and feeling. To lose a father and not know why. Of course, he wasn't really gone yet. They visited him on Sundays, driving the twenty miles north to the only hospice in the metro area that had been able to take him. But he wasn't really there either. He had gained a lot of weight, grown a beard, forgotten who they were.

Oh, once in a while, he would show up and say "I love you" to his wife or "how's school?" to one of the braver children who would stand by his bed. But before they could answer, he'd be gone again. Inside himself. Trapped in a brain that no longer made all the right connections.

There was almost more of him now on a piece of celluloid than in real life. No wonder Julie could sit and watch the video for so long. It was all she really had of the man she used to call Daddy, who used to tuck her in at night, who used to mow their lawn and shovel their sidewalk. Who used to come home every night after work, take off his tie and put on his workout clothes. He'd either get on the stationary bike or go to the rec center, but he'd always take care of himself.

Yet he had known he would die young. He often talked about his father's early death. And his uncles'. He once told his mother that he had to work hard, he couldn't slow down, he had to provide for his family because he had so little time. But who knew how little he had?

Lisa and the kids had tried to celebrate his thirty-fourth birthday with him in June. He had not understood. Jamie opened the presents on his lap, showed them to him, explained what they were, who they were from. He had not responded. They tried so hard to reach him, but he was like a character in a movie that one can only watch.

So I knew that somehow this video was good for Julie, helping her to see the change in her daddy, to realize it, to accept it, and then to go on with her play. Although it made me uncomfortable. The same way that taking her mom to the movie *Legends of the Fall* would make me feel that winter...

Somehow scenes of funerals with snow-covered mountains in the background helped her with her grief, but I could only remember her husband's burial a few weeks before on a clear, cold, windy Montana day.

I wanted to say, "Let's get out of here, go out, have a little fun!"

It was New Year's Day on the video now and the family was eating turkey. I had fed them turkey, too, almost a year ago, on their first Thanksgiving in Denver. Bob, I can say his name now, had insisted on taking the pictures, so he's not in them.

The rest of us are sitting around the table, smiling at the camera, thankful for the blessings in our lives, for food, for friends, for children, for each other.

"Babysitter," Julie says (yes, she calls me that), "it's over." I realize I am crying, but quickly wipe my tears away with my hand.

"Okay," I say. "Do you want me to rewind it so you can watch it another day?" "Yes," she nods, and she climbs off my lap and heads for the Legos.

Bob died of Creutzfeldt-Jacob disease (CJD), more commonly known as mad cow disease. He either contracted it through steroids (derived from cadavers) he took for his acne when he was a teenager, or through eating foods such as monkey brains in the very rural areas of China when he was there on business.

His widow, Lisa, has gone on with her life, returning to college while taking care of three children at home and one in an institution. She is also an aerobics instructor and works part-time at a department store. She just recently remarried after almost six years on her own, seven if one counts the year Bob was ill.

Independent at Heart
by Margaret Anne Wright

Maureen opened her eyes and looked over at the partially draped window of her hospital room. She could see the sun rising over the city skyline. Even though she still felt tired, she pressed the lever on the side of her bed to lift her upper body. The nurse had told her to shower, so she took the starched white towel and clean hospital gown off the small dented gray metal night stand. Her lungs ached. She sat for a moment and rested.

Maureen was lucky, at age thirty-six, to have parents who cared for her. When she had moved out of their house at nineteen, she never thought she would be dependent on them again. Yet they needed her as much as she needed them. Shortly after she moved home, her mother was diagnosed with Parkinson's disease.

Barefoot and clad in only a light blue gown, she slowly shuffled to the open door. The hallway was dark and empty. She paused for a moment to catch her breath before continuing across the hall to the shower room.

Fidgeting with the stiff nozzle, Maureen pointed it away from her so that she wouldn't get a blast of cold water. She tested the temperature of the water with her hand, and as it warmed, allowed it to flow over her. She loved how it soothed her sore muscles. She began lathering shampoo through her hair, suddenly grasping for breath and putting the palm of her hand against the shower stall.

Brad, an old boyfriend, suddenly popped into her head. She hadn't thought of him in years. Maybe your whole life does flash before your eyes during times of trauma.

They had just finished supper at his townhouse. When she rose to wash the dishes, he asked, "Why do you have to do the dishes now?"

She looked at him. "I have the energy now."

"I'd like you to do them later," he told her. Maureen put the red plaid dishcloth on the counter. "Okay, I'll do them later." She didn't know why he was making an issue out of such a small task.

Then when she was nearly asleep in front of the TV, Brad said, "Now it's time to do the dishes." She didn't feel like washing the dishes, but she got up anyway.

Wrapping her towel around her wet hair, Maureen took a bottle of iodine as instructed and squirted it all over her body. She caught her breath, leaned against the chipped wooden bathroom door, and shut her eyes. When her dizziness subsided, she donned her clean gown. Opening the door to the hallway, she heard the chatter of nurses. She rested her head against the cold metal frame just for a moment.

When Maureen was dating Travis a couple years ago, she hadn't realized she was so deathly ill. The doctors had assured her that nothing was wrong. So she exhausted herself trying to keep up with Travis. But just trying to walk with him was hard even though his pace was slow. Twice he had said, "Why would anyone want to be with someone who is sick?" Both times, Maureen thought he was talking about his rheumatoid arthritis; she hadn't known how to respond.

Maureen managed her way into bed and had just closed her eyes when the phone rang. Rolling over, she reached for the receiver before the third ring.

"How are you?" asked her brother.

"Okay, I had a wonderful night's sleep, thanks to the sleeping pills." She laid back on the pillow, the phone next to her ear.

"That's good," he replied. Then an uncomfortable silence.

"You must be busy studying for your exam," Maureen said.

"Not really. I know most of the stuff."

"Then you'll Ace it," she almost whispered.

There was nothing left to talk about except the one topic that neither of them wanted to mention—her heart surgery.

"This is it," her brother finally said.

"Yeah," Maureen responded. "The day I've fought so hard to see."

A tall middle-aged man with a white uniform knocked on her open door. "Are you Miss Sanders?" he asked.

Maureen held her hand over the receiver. "Yes."

"I've come to take you downstairs."

"I'll just say good-bye to my brother."

"That's okay," replied the man. "I have a few minutes."

Maureen was relieved he was understanding, yet she knew he was probably busy, so didn't want to keep him too long. "A man is here to wheel me downstairs," she told her brother.

"I love you," he mumbled, a first for him.

"I'll see you next week at home," said Maureen. She had no intention of dying. She was a survivor.

She heard a sob before hanging up. "I'm ready," she told the man.

She settled herself on the black, narrow stretcher. The lights were on in the hallway now and the glare from the old circular tubes hurt her eyes. She shut them and could feel herself rolling toward her one chance to live.

Maureen had been near death a number of times. The worst was with her cousin at her aunt's cottage by the lake. They were there for a whole week to relax and enjoy the sun. But on Wednesday morning when Maureen was swimming at the beach, her heartbeat went irregular and started racing. She knew from previous experiences of atrial fibrillation that if she didn't get help right away, she could have a blood clot that would result in a stroke. Taking three steps at a time, then resting, she managed to walk up the hill to where her cousin was watching TV.

"I need to go to the emergency room."

"I'm watching my soap opera," her cousin replied, not even glancing her way.

Maureen was unsure whether her cousin had heard her. "I need to go to the emergency room," she repeated, a little louder. "There's something wrong with my heart."

"I said I'm watching my program!" her cousin actually yelled.

Maureen was helpless. There was no phone and no car. She didn't have the energy to argue, only to drag herself to the nearest chair at the dining room table.

Twenty minutes later, her cousin turned off the TV. "Now what did you want?"

"Could you get someone to drive me to the emergency room?"

Her cousin pranced into the kitchen. "You can't expect someone to just drop what they're doing just because you have a heart problem. You expect way too much."

It would be three days, yes, three days, before someone came by with a car and Maureen asked them to take her to the hospital. Three days of wondering how much damage this time.

The man wheeled her through the double doors. He stopped to grab a light blue cap and pulled it over his black curls. "Don't I get a hat?" She asked.

"Not to worry, Miss," he answered, handing her one.

"Now I can be in Vogue," Maureen said, pushing her hair underneath the elastic.

The man chuckled. "Your sense of humor will get you through this."

He left her in front of the nurses' station.

Maureen shut her eyes while a nurse checked her blood pressure. She could feel the blood rushing through her veins; she could feel herself floating. She crossed her arms over her chest to keep from falling off the narrow bed. A few minutes later, she awoke wondering if it was all over. Realizing it was not, she closed her eyes again, trying to sleep. She hated the wait.

Then feeling her gurney move, she opened her eyes and saw two nurses.

"It's time," one of them said.

Maureen nodded and closed her eyes again. She heard the sound of doors being pushed open. When the gurney stopped, she opened her eyes for just a second to very bright lights. She was shifted onto a cold table. Someone pulled her arms out of the gown, then lay it on top of her. Another attendant strapped her arms to the narrow table. She felt the pain of a needle enter her left wrist.

Maureen went to sleep feeling privileged that she was getting another chance at life. Historically, people with her problem died. In third world countries, people with her problem still died. By all laws of nature, she should have died, but somehow she was still alive.

After her surgery, after her recovery, in her new life, if she were to survive, she knew she would have to stay away from controlling, selfish people. She would have to be as independent as her heart would allow, staying close to the family members that had loved and cared for her, choosing her friends carefully, and never, ever again taking her life for granted.

Her Best Day
by Debbie Simms

Psychological battery—a new concept, yet definitely an old reality. It's just as damaging as physical abuse, but overlooked since it's not as visible. It resides in the heart and soul, in the very psyche of its victim...

Looking back, Debbie could see how she had gotten to this place, the pit of low self-esteem. Her mother used to rattle off Debbie's shortcomings on a regular basis. Her haircut, for one, accentuated her less-than-perfect nose. How could she even think about bringing attention to something that unattractive? It wasn't cute and perky, so it must be ugly, right? Yeah, right.

Then there were the banjo lessons. Debbie always wanted to play bluegrass, and her parents agreed to pay for lessons. She progressed from the start, learning to pick to the beat with her quick nimble fingers.

Then one day her mom came to get her. She hadn't known that the store manager had hired one of Debbie's classmates to teach her the banjo, and couldn't believe the two girls weren't just goofing off, spending the whole hour talking about boys. Wasting time and money. The lessons were cancelled without any discussion. And that was the end of that.

Debbie grew up in the country near a small town in Colorado. She was always athletic, and she loved the outdoors, the blue sky framing white-topped mountains, the air crisp and clear. Running around in the fields, hunting in the mountains, chasing the horses, running with the family dog, it was just a matter of time before Debbie started running for the fun of it.

One day during gym class, the track coach watched Debbie run the hurdles, then took her aside. "Would you be interested in joining the track team?" Debbie was thrilled! How exciting to be asked by the coach! She ran from the school bus to tell her parents.

Her mistake was not waiting for her dad to come home, but it probably wouldn't have made a difference. Without hesitation her mom just said, "No, I need you to come straight home everyday to unload the dishwasher." Debbie turned and, slumping her shoulders, shuffled down the stairs to her cold room in the basement.

"I could have gotten a scholarship," she would think years later. "But instead I never went to college. I might have gone to the Olympics and won a gold medal. Or played the banjo in some famous band, becoming a world-renowned musician."

But she'd never know, realizing her chance had come and gone. It was too late…

Then Debbie followed her boyfriend to New York City and eventually got married. Boy, could that man run her down into the ground. Everything about her needed improving. She shouldn't wear heels with jeans, but should wear clothes that he found sexy, rather than clothes she liked. She didn't read enough, didn't know enough, wasn't academic enough. The meals she prepared after working all day could always be better, and even at five feet, seven inches and only 125 pounds, she was too heavy, lumpy in all the wrong places.

Worst of all, every chance he got, he put her down in front of others. When Debbie asked him why he said, "I figure if I do it enough, you'll eventually change."

One day, after three years of marriage and thank God no children, Debbie couldn't take it any more. Something just snapped. She was no longer willing to accept his behavior.

It must have been survival instinct, for she hadn't planned it. She hadn't even realized she was that desperate. But in an instant, it was over. And she left him.

The worst part was not the loneliness, for she preferred being alone to being under attack. Nor was it her lack of financial stability, having walked out without even her wedding china. No, the worst part was her feeling like a failure.

She had been taught that divorce was wrong, very wrong, and she had honestly thought it would never happen to her. Anyone else, but not to her. What a dope! Did she think she was above it all? That she should be able to make her husband happy? Able to be what he wanted?

Now she was in the same boat as other people, women at work, at church, whose marriages, whose dreams, had faded away. What an idiot she was! Her husband and her mother were right—she was a failure. She needed to change. And until she did, she would never be valuable…

Even in her misery, even in her pain, there was one thing Debbie had never given up. She still loved to run. She could run where she wanted, when she wanted, and for as long as she wanted. The freedom of running made her spirits soar. Endorphins they call it, but it was her escape—from the sameness, the doubts, the other- and self-imposed shame. While running, she was independent. She was a success. She liked herself.

So after leaving her husband, she ran even more. Whenever she could. Whenever she needed to feel better. Even if that was three in the morning, when fear would wake her and her mind would need to wander, away from her bedroom, her apartment, her empty life, her failures as a person.

Running after midnight in a big city, alone, is unwise, especially for a woman. But Debbie didn't care. She ran anyway. She ran in the dark. She ran in the rain. It didn't matter that she lived in a seedy neighborhood. It didn't matter that men were driving up and down the streets looking for those women who "want a ride."

How many times did a car pull over and ask her if she "wanted a ride"? It didn't matter. It just didn't matter. All that mattered was running. Escape. So her soul would be free, at least for a while, from her own mental beatings...

After months of running in the dark at all times of the night, something inside Debbie made her really wake up, as if she had been sleepwalking. A quiet healing started to seep into her consciousness. She began to see herself for the person she really was, not the one her mother and husband had pointed out in their mirrors. Debbie began to forgive herself for having listened to them, for believing them.

Somewhere in the night, somewhere in the dark, somewhere in her fleeing, God, she believes, delivered her. Perhaps it was the endorphins that told her to open her eyes one night as she waited for a light to change, just in time to see a shape looming in the distance. Who was out there? Why were they up so late? Were they waiting for her?

What was she doing out here in the dark, alone? She could get hurt. She could get killed!

When the light changed, Debbie didn't resume her run. Instead, she simply turned around and walked quickly back to her apartment. "I don't want to get killed," she thought. "I don't want to get hurt. I want to go home and take care of myself. I am worth saving. I am valuable."

Debbie didn't give up running. She just stopped going out in the middle of the night. She joined hiking groups, took up cycling, and learned to be assertive at work—getting the private office she needed to get her work done.

She said "no" to the relatives who wanted her to come home for the holidays if she didn't want to, without making big excuses.

She spent money on concerts and the opera and Broadway shows. She went by herself if no one could go. Sometimes, she just went by herself, not even stopping to ask anyone.

But she never took dangerous risks again, just the healthy kind. The kind that makes one grow and flourish and be content with life. The kind that say, *I am worth it, I am lovable, I am me!*

A Warrior Woman's Path
by Colleen Flanagan

The phone rang at the usual time, yet I hesitated before picking it up. I knew who it was. He wanted an answer and wasted no time after we'd exchanged polite greetings.

"Have you given any more thought to moving to Asia with me?"

"Yes," I replied, then took a deep breath. "And the answer is still no."

"I'll eventually get you to say yes, so you might as well say it now." A deep chuckle echoed all the way from Thailand to Arizona. "We're soul mates and belong together. I'm moving overseas, and so are you. Case closed."

My rebellious nature bristled at his matter-of-fact smugness. I heard muffled, accented voices in the background and knew he was calling from work. He was always working.

"Hold on," he said. "The operations group needs help."

While my road warrior lover assisted clients in a computer room halfway across the globe, I dealt with the sick twisting of my stomach. The take-charge attitude I'd found so sexy in him now felt threatening. The kind, committed person I'd fallen for months ago had been replaced by this overpowering man who often changed our plans on his own whims, rarely consulting me. Even worse, I suspected that this new persona was the real him. After we'd met, he'd discovered what kind of a man I wanted in my life and then pretended to be him. Once I'd fallen in love, he began the slow, silent process of seizing all the power in our relationship.

My journaling over the last few weeks had helped me uncover the reasons for the niggling anxiety haunting me night and day. I'd always been an independent, assertive woman, yet at times this man treated me like a disobedient wife. Instead of arguing, I found it easier to go along with his agenda. The slow erosion of my power both disgusted and frightened me.

Did I have the courage to discuss my fears with him? "Go ahead and get it off your chest," my mind taunted. "What's the worst that can happen?" The scared, little girl inside answered immediately. "He'll abandon me to pursue his adventures. If he really is my soul mate, I'll have lost what could have been my last opportunity for real love…"

When he returned to the phone, I took a long sip from my coffee cup and spoke.

"Remember when you said that I could tell you anything?" At his assent, I continued. "I haven't been feeling real good about 'us' lately, and have done a lot of soul searching. It seems that you find your self-worth in hunting and conquering people or things you find challenging. Like all those businesses you started, made a lot of money at, then sold because you got bored with them."

"There's nothing wrong with that."

"I agree. But, now that you've conquered me, and I'm in love with you, you're moving on to another challenge, in Asia."

"I'm a road warrior. That's my nature. You were meant to be by my side as my mate, my warrior woman. Our paths have merged and we must now walk together. In Asia."

"I don't want to leave Arizona. I've told you that from the start." (Then why is that sick, guilty feeling churning in my gut? Isn't it my duty to leave my family and friends to live in a foreign country with my soul mate?)

Still holding the phone to my left ear, I opened my patio door and walked into the warm morning air. The mad chatter of hummingbirds fighting over the feeder in my backyard made it difficult to think. A gecko darted across my path and up the stucco wall. I couldn't leave this magnificent state I'd called home for twenty years, but how could I explain this to him?

"This is the only place I've really felt comfortable." I tried to appeal to his compassionate nature. "Like any desert creature, I'd wither and die if I was taken from my natural habitat."

"Nonsense. Like me, you're a survivor. You should be willing to travel with me, and hang your shingle below mine. There's a quarter of a million dollars a year to be made in a virtually inexhaustible market over here..."

My mind drifted and I half-listened as he extolled the benefits of our move to Asia. Where did he get the notion that I'd pick up and follow him anywhere? The only moving we'd agreed upon was to a small town north of Phoenix, where he'd work from home as a software consultant, and I could write full-time. And what was this shingle-hanging crap?

Life had been so much simpler before this emotional roller coaster called "us." The intense love—or was it infatuation?—kept me on an ecstatic high, but I hadn't been able to write anything except journal entries. My novel and potential magazine articles sat neglected on my hard drive while I waited each day for my overseas love to call. I was letting the present slip by while I daydreamed about "our" future.

"...I might be able to get you a job, too. What do you think?"

"I think my shingle will only hang *below* yours. You used to refer to us as a team. It seems that you've quietly elected yourself the boss."

"I'm the older, more experienced one. My shingle must hang on top. And alone."

He spoke to me as an adult would admonish a child, and I felt angry. As a forty-four-year-old, self-made, professional woman, I expected nothing less than mutual respect from this person who claimed to be my true love. Hesitant to speak in anger, I remained speechless.

"Are you there?"

"Yes," I replied. "I'm thinking about what you said and—"

"Hold on," he interrupted. "I've got to check out a problem on a disk drive. In the meantime, why don't you think about how great it would be to live here with me."

With a clunk of the telephone receiver, he was gone again.

His confident words had me picturing him grinning with that classic "I win again" look on his face. An aggressive entrepreneur, he conducted his life like a giant chess game, using real people as pawns. Conquest, his beloved Queen. I knew I would never dethrone her. The futility of the situation struck me solidly. I had no right to tell him how to run his life, nor had he any right to rule mine.

The sun's warmth seeped through my clothes, relaxing my shoulders and back. I peered up at the clear blue desert sky. Freedom or security? Which will it be? A life here with myself, or as a road warrior's woman, traveling and living in hotels while he achieves his next triumph? And what about my triumphs? Had I been fooling myself that this romance would work? Was I too blind in love to see that his offer of financial security, of being "taken care of" came with a ball and chain? Was I desperate enough to nurse it along, or brave enough to let it die, as it surely would?

The phone receiver clattered at his end, and I heard him barking orders to his "pawns."

"I've gotta go, the system crashed." Sheer excitement resonated in his voice. Another coup, another potential conquest, another call to action.

I'd had enough.

"I've gotta go, too." My words came out in a whisper; then the warrior woman within me spoke boldly. "Permanently."

"What's that supposed to mean?"

"If you ever get tired of finding your self-worth in the outside world and want to live in Arizona, give me a call. If I'm available, we'll see how we feel about each other then."

"Are you dumping me? I can't believe you're dumping me."

"I can't believe you thought you could change everything we'd agreed upon and expect me not to call you on it." I caressed the golden velvet petals of a tender jasmine blossom. So fragile, so easily destroyed, yet strong enough to thrive on it's own in the desert.

"You're throwing away the love of your life, your warrior, your soul mate!"

"Maybe. Our time together was an experience I'll never forget. Thank you for helping me recognize *my* warrior woman." I felt a tiny grin tug at the corners of my mouth. "She's become great friends with and the protector of my inner child." His stunned silence energized me. I was reclaiming my power, for the first time in months. "The difference between you and me is that I'm trying to conquer the challenges within me first. You're looking to the outside world, when there's still much to be done within."

"This isn't the end," he growled. "I won't let it end like this."

"You have no choice. It's over." Hearing my own words and admitting the truth out loud hurt. I swallowed the lump in my throat. I'd be sobbing soon, and didn't want him to know my pain. "Good-bye and good luck."

I pressed the TALK button on my cordless phone, immediately severing our connection.

A dull ache constricted my chest and I forced myself to deeply inhale the warm, calming desert air. I was alone again.

I walked slowly down the meandering, tiled path of my meditation garden, past lush green jasmine vines awash in yellow flowers, pristine white daisies and lavender rose bushes. I plucked a daisy and tucked it behind my right ear.

Alone again. It wasn't a bad thing at all.

About the Editors

Dianne Lorang was first inspired to collect stories about and by single women when she realized they had something she did not. Having been married over twenty years at the time, she thought the strength and happiness of her single friends and relatives came from their independence. She discovered, instead, that contentment and fulfillment come from deep within a person rather than from one's present or past circumstances.

After much therapy and journal writing, Ms. Lorang was able to achieve the knowledge that she could remain in a relationship and yet rely on herself at the same time. "It's an attitude," she says. "It's not an 'open marriage.' My husband and I consult each other about finances, share in decisions, make plans together, but often go on separate vacations." They have three grown children and live in Littleton, Colorado.

Prior to starting The Write Help in 1996, Ms. Lorang was a Literary Assistant at Jody Rein Books. She has edited a variety of books, including *The ADDed Dimension: Everyday Advice for Adults with ADD,* by Kate Kelly, Peggy Ramundo, and D. Steven Ledingham (Scribner, 1997); *Mother of the Pound: Memoirs of the Life and History of the Iraqi Jews,* by David Kazzaz (Sepher Hermon Press, 1999); *The Practice of Wholeness,* by Lorena Monda (Golden Flower Publications, 2000); and *Saving the Bay: People Working for the Future of the Chesapeake*, by Ann E. Byrnes and Richard A. K. Dorbin (The Johns Hopkins University Press, 2001).

She also edited short stories for Patricia Henley's latest book, *Worship of the Common Heart* (MacMurray & Beck, 2000). Ms. Lorang received her education at Montana State University, where she began honing her editorial skills as a Professional Tutor at the Writing Center.

Ann E. Byrnes was one of the first contributors to *Single Women – Alive and Well!* with her story, "Seventh Inning Stretch," about learning to cope in a college chemistry class at the age of thirty-eight. She and editor Dianne Lorang became friends via the Internet and have been able to visit in person on occasion.

I

Dianne Lorang and Ann E. Byrnes

They worked closely together on Ms. Byrnes' book, *Saving the Bay: People Working for the Future of the Chesapeake* (The Johns Hopkins University Press, 2001). "This is a book about hope, rather than despair," says Andrew R. McCown, Echo Hill Outdoor School. "Yes, humans create tremendous problems, but we also have the capability to solve them."

Ms. Byrnes' present partner in business and life, Richard A. K. Dorbin, created the photography for *Saving the Bay: People Working for the Future of the Chesapeake*. They live on Maryland's Eastern Shore.

Ms. Byrnes' hobbies include swimming, bike riding, gardening, and listening to folk music. Before joining the ranks of non-traditional students, she worked extensively in the construction and finance industries.

Having written for business and pleasure most of her life, including essays, short stories, children's stories, and poetry, Ms. Byrnes has won several writing awards and been published in many local and university periodicals. Along with her own publishing success, she pens book proposals for other authors and designs web-sites.

She will have earned her B.S. in Behavioral and Social Sciences with a minor in Communications from the University of Maryland University College in 2002, all while continuing to work and raise two young children, mostly on her own. Two more of Ms. Byrnes' stories—"Mirrorstones" and "Welcome the Seasons"— appear in *Single Women – Alive and Well!*

About Our Writers
(alphabetical by first names)

CeLeste Lee grew up in New Mexico surrounded by Indian Reservations and has a book in the works about a Navajo Indian. She moved to Texas in 1984 and says she "loves the weather." Fresh out of high school, she worked for a construction company as a receptionist, working her way up to secretary-treasurer of their building division. She left that position to start a family, but after her husband's death, opened a convenience store and café.

After thirteen years, she sold them and started substitute teaching. She also began keeping a daily journal with the idea of writing a book later. Ms. Lee presently works in a school for emotionally disturbed and learning disabled middle-school children, as well as mentally handicapped adults who need job placement.

Much to her surprise, she says, she remarried last year after "not dating for seven years and being perfectly happy with her single status." She now has ten children, two sons-in-law, and four grandchildren.

Chandra K. Clarke is a freelance writer and author living in a rural portion of Southwestern Ontario, Canada. She started her career by tromping through corn fields and cattle barns in search of stories for the local agricultural press. When she's not flogging her vast portfolio of soybean articles, she provides copy and content to international publications like *Homes & Cottages* and *Discovery Channel Online*. If pressed, she'll admit that she's also done hard time as a municipal beat reporter and a managing editor for a weekly newspaper.

She has a B.A. in English and Psychology, and is currently working on a M.Sc. in Space Studies. She is the author of the popular humor column, "In My Humble Opinion" (www.chandrakclarke.com), the non-fiction book, *Humor Writing: The Art of Being Funny* (booklocker.com, 1999), and a sci-fi novel, *Taiamoora* (Xlibris Corporation, 2000). *It Came From Planet Neefnoof*, a collection of her past columns, is coming out in 2001.

You can find out more about Ms. Clarke as well as "Planet Neefnoof" at www.chandrakclarke.com/aboutme.htm.

Colleen Flanagan, lured as a teenager by the mysterious beauty of the desert, has lived most of her blissfully single adult life in Arizona. A business analyst consultant and technical writer by trade, she spends much of her free time on her soul's passion—writing. Her non-fiction articles about the single life and personal experiences have appeared in magazines and newspapers nationwide.

Although raised to be a good Midwestern wife and mother, Ms. Flanagan's life's goals changed when at age nineteen, she watched Scarlett O'Hara overcome all odds in the classic movie, *Gone with the Wind.* Fired with new determination and the knowledge that women can be as strong and independent as men, Ms. Flanagan worked her way into becoming the first female software engineer in two groups at Honeywell.

Currently, she is finishing her first novel, *Thunderstruck,* under the watchful eye of her significant other, a Siamese Fighting Fish (*betta splendens*) named Cujo.

Debbie Simms is a "fairly easy-going gal" who likes to spend time hiking, camping, listening to music, playing the piano, reading, petting her cat, hanging out with friends, and generally enjoying life. She grew up in a rural community in Colorado, but as the result of a short marriage, wound up in New York City. "Over the years," she says, "I've learned to maintain a small town philosophy even in this big metropolis."

She works as an administrator at a large university, a job with a great deal of responsibility and contact with people from around the country, yet a laid-back atmosphere derived from a mixture of students, faculty, and staff, which Ms. Simms says is "good for me." She attended college for a few years before learning her real world skills at a vocational and trade school.

She has no children, but has never had a problem with regret. She echoes what a lot of strong and happy unmarried women have said: "Although I am not opposed to finding 'Mr. Right,' I thoroughly enjoy the green grass on the single side of the fence."

Debbie Tomasovic inhabited many different houses before making her home in St. Petersburg, Florida. As a military daughter, she repeatedly was the "new kid on the block." Her mother told her, "As we travel through life, we will be most fortunate to have literally gathered just a handful of 'real friends' by the end of our journey." It took Ms. Tomasovic quite a few years to appreciate the truth of that statement.

She counts her mother amongst her cherished 'real friends' who have blessed her with their ever-supportive presence. She believes her mother's message implied that there is no one better suited to care for our own needs than ourselves. "Everyone else is but icing on the proverbial cake."

As a family therapist, Ms. Tomasovic counsels survivors of child sexual abuse. She loves nature and plays often with her mountain bike, named "Towanda," from *Fried Green Tomatoes,* and her kayak, named *Guia,* Spanish for "pathfinder." She says that her "fiercely funny female friends," courageous clients, and the natural rhythms of Mother Earth inspire her writing.

Dora Marjorie is the pen name of Lillian-Rose Thomas, an Australian who has lived in New Zealand for thirty years. "Retiring by nature," at eighty years old, she has enjoyed a long life in music and literature. She attributes her literary interests to the ballad, "George and Sarah Green" by William Wordsworth, and a journal, *The Greens of Grassmere,* by Dorothy Wordsworth, both telling the story of the rescue of the Greens' children by the Wordsworths in 1808. Hannah Green, a baby at the time, was Ms. Marjorie's (Thomas') great-great-grandmother.

Although Ms. Marjorie calls herself an "elderly lady of leisure," claiming she "pats the dog, cooks, reads, and enjoys good television drama," she and her husband own and run Edtext International (edtext@xtra.co.nz) which edits and rewrites research papers and books, mainly for Asian academics as well as a cancer institute in Europe. She finds the Internet a "wonderful machine for this sort of work."

On occasion, she and her husband attend auctions searching for bargains of the "Abagail" variety. "Abagail" is her first story published internationally.

Ellen Kurtz has worked as a teacher, lecturer, feature writer, and newspaper and magazine editor since 1955, when she graduated from Brooklyn College. Her articles, self-syndicated columns, and reviews have appeared in over 200 publications. She has conducted workshops and moderated panel discussions at writers' conferences, and given speeches on her craft at colleges and public forums.

As the last writer to interview and photograph noted sculptor Natan Rapoport just two weeks before his death in 1987, Ms. Kurtz is often invited to lecture and write about him and his work, as well as other sculptors and their monuments and museum pieces. An active member of New Jersey Press Women (an affiliate of the National Federation of Press Women), she was named their New Jersey Communicator of Achievement for 1997. She is listed in several editions of *Who's Who* for her work in journalism.

A grandmother, Ms. Kurtz is making another transition as she moves with her new life partner to an "active adult 55+" community in Rockaway Township, New Jersey.

Gail E. Parsons, R.N., M.A., CACII, is a native of Ontario, Canada, but has lived in the United States for over thirty years, almost twenty of those in Colorado, where she moved shortly after becoming a citizen. She received her nursing degree from St. Thomas Elgin General Hospital in Ontario, and then worked as an R.N. in Barbados, West Indies, before finding work in Michigan, where she married and had three children.

She returned to school in 1983 and earned her B.A. and M.A. degrees from Regis University in Denver, training as a Certified Family Therapist, a Certified Addiction Counselor (CACII), and an approved domestic violence counselor. She has worked in the addictions field as a Masters Level Therapist in the Denver metro area since 1990.

Her three children are in their twenties and also live in Colorado. Ms. Parsons' interests include photography, walking, water aerobics, and art appreciation.

Jan Neville is an award-winning speaker and storyteller, best known in Toastmasters for her "Tall Tale." Her three-act biographical play, *Elizabeth Palmer Peabody,* was performed by sixty elementary school students, ages five to twelve years old. One scene depicting her heroine's strength was shown on the *Noell and Andy Television Show*.

Born in Chicago, Ms. Neville is a long-time resident of Centennial, Colorado. Her education includes a B.A. in Theatre, an M.A. in Library Science, and a Ph.D. in Speech Communication, all from the University of

Denver. She has taught kindergarten through high school, as well as been a public school librarian and media specialist.

Currently, she serves the Denver area as a theatre archivist, performing "drive-by pick-ups" of theatre programs and posters for posterity.

Lana Book began writing when she was twelve years old, starting with a "syrupy sweet" poem about a boy she had a crush on at school. It has only taken her forty years to learn that life "just isn't that serious." She likes to intertwine fiction and non-fiction, she says, to "add mystery" to her writing. She has had short stories, poems, and essays published in two other anthologies, *Coming Full Circle* (Plain View Press, 1997) and *Pink Macaroni Flamingo* (Quill Merchants, her weekly critique group).

A resident of the great state of Texas, Ms. Book has had four essays printed in the *San Antonio Express News*, and five children's stories in *The Cowboy Express*. She enjoys sponsoring and hosting writing workshops and poetry readings, sometimes with concerts, at her home in Kerrville, Texas, surrounded by eighteen acres she has named The Hill Country Sculpture and Meditation Garden.

She also welcomes guests into her home, the Elm Cottage Bed & Breakfast found at www.wkcc.com/ElmCottage.htm. She can be reached at elmcott@ktc.com.

Lisa Minassian joined the Marine Corps in the middle of her college career. She served most of her term in Okinawa, Japan, and has had several of her personal experience stories from that time published in *Tropities*, *Orato*, and *Women's International Network* magazines.

Her grandmother's stories about growing up in an orphanage in Syria after the Armenian genocide, as well as her strength and love of life without bitterness, inspired her to get through boot camp. Her mother has always encouraged her to make her own decisions, "whether they're right or wrong," and supported her through them.

After graduating from college, Ms. Minassian moved to Paris and traveled around Europe before returning to her native Massachusetts to open a cozy bookstore in Reading. It was there, meeting with local writers, that she began writing herself. Recently married, Ms. Minassian and her husband, Eric Cordeiro, are renovating a rowhouse in Watertown, Massachusetts. They are expecting their first child in April.

Mariah Lancaster has lived in Maine since she was eight years old. Although only writing for about ten years, she has been "wildly working on story lines since that time." Her mind, she says, wrote the following long before it wound its way through her fingers:

> *My brother and I were sitting bareback on our horses; the white creatures suddenly decided to take a jog through the nearby woods. As I clung tightly to the strands of my horse's mane, terror stepped aside while I carefully memorized everything: how the warm breeze tried to tear my legs away from the horse's belly, and how the gait of my brother's horse broke the consistency of his panicked cries.*

Ms. Lancaster works as a reporter and staff writer for *The Star-Herald*, a weekly newspaper in Presque Isle, Maine. She freelances "when time permits" and is also working on her first novel, *Above All Else*, about a woman who learns about her own strength and determination after her husband dies weeks before her baby is born.

Ms. Lancaster has been blessed with one more child since the writing of "My Son, My Strength."

Margaret Anne Wright obtained a B.A. in English at York University, Toronto, Ontario, Canada. She also earned two writing certificates from the Institute of Children's Literature of Pennsylvania, one in Writing for Children and Teenagers, and the other in Beyond the Basics. Since having a mitral valve replacement, Ms. Wright was diagnosed with a deadly illness—pulmonary hypertension. She continues to live as independently as possible while meeting the challenges of her debilitating disease.

The women she most admires are her Internet friends who also suffer from pulmonary hypertension and manage the disease by themselves. Women who spend forty-five minutes washing a bathtub with their bare feet because they would faint if they had to wash the tub using their hands. Women who must mix their flolan drug with precision and timeliness or else die. Women who wake up alone in their homes after being unconscious for hours or even days. Some women who never woke up…

"Independent at Heart" is Ms. Wright's first published story. She lives in Peterborough, Ontario.

Marilyn Farber Jacobs lives in New York City and in Palm Beach County, Florida. She is a lifetime member of the North Tulsa Literary Guild which published her poem, "To Be or Not to Be a Friend," in their Spring 1999 issue of *Poetry Protocol*. It also appeared in the *Merseyside Arts Monthly* in England. Other poems by Ms. Farber Jacobs are in Hidden Book Press anthologies and online in the *Amateur Poetry Journal*.

She says she no longer waits for a man to buy her gifts or take her to fabulous places, but rather treats herself the way she would want to be treated. She is "owned" by her Bengal cat, Chutney, who is five generations from a baby leopard, and the subject of several of her poems.

Pat Wulle's story, "Crossing Lost Trail," was the inspiration for *Single Women – Alive and Well!* She is the first cousin of editor Dianne Lorang's mother. A native of Missoula, Montana, Ms. Wulle lives in Salt Lake City, Utah, presently sharing her home with her oldest son who had a heart attack last year. Her two other sons live close by with their families and keep her entertained with their antics. (One of her grandsons is named Wilden, so his name is "Wild 'n' Wooly.")

She spent twenty-eight years as a secretary for Hercules Aerospace until taking medical leave in 1989 when diagnosed with lymphoma. She has undergone chemotherapy three times but is doing very well, attending aerobics and Tai Chi classes, and also volunteering at the State Library for the Blind.

She took a walking tour of the Alps and another of Hawaii, plus has traveled to Tahiti, Bermuda, Spain, New York City (a big deal for a country girl), and Alaska.

Sharon Eberhardt writes part-time from her home in Brantford, Ontario, Canada, and has published several short stories in magazines and on the Internet. She wrote "Tightwired" in hopes of reaching not only victims of vertigo, to give them faith that there is, indeed, life after this dreadful condition, but to tell women everywhere to "go forth and conquer" whatever obstacle is in their way.

"All it takes is courage and determination," she tells them. "Love yourself as you would your child. You are worth it. Life can be wonderful if we give to ourselves what we would give to others."

She is expecting her second grandchild and has nothing but gratitude that she can be there in mind, body, and spirit for her daughter, who has always been there for her. Ms. Eberhardt wishes to dedicate "Tightwired" to her friend Helen, who has helped her through the bleakest periods of her life, as well as to the Internet support group, *Dizzinews*.

"They gave me hope when there was none," she says. "I shall not forget those brave, wonderful souls!"

Veronica Shoffstall's poem, "After a While," has been published in some thirty books, including Ann Landers' *Wake Up and Smell the Coffee* (Random House, 1996), two of the *Chicken Soup for the Soul* books (Health Communications), and *The Language of Recovery* (Blue Mountain Arts Press, 2000). Several of her other poems have appeared in more obscure publications as well as on the Internet.

A native of Astoria, New York, Ms. Shoffstall has a B.A. in Sociology, and a Certificate in Journalism from New York University. She lives in New York City where she works on a newsletter reporting the activities of Baha'i communities from around the world. As a member of the Baha'I Faith, she believes that God created all people noble, and that all humankind is one single race.

Her life companion for the moment is "one very timid" cat.

Our Writers Recommend

AUTHORS

♦ Alice Walker

♦ Ann Rivers Siddons

♦ Bell Hooks

♦ Catherine Cookson

♦ Charlotte and Emily Bronte

♦ Luanne Rice

♦ L.M. (Lucy Maud) Montgomery

♦ Marilyn French

♦ Maya Angelou

♦ Rod Serling

♦ Sarah Orne Jewett

BOOKS

♦ *A Language in Common,* by Marion Molteno (reprinted in New Zealand by Addenda Ltd: ed.nz@xtra.co.nz)

♦ *A Shield of Coolest Air,* by Marion Molteno (Shola Books, 1992)

Dianne Lorang and Ann E. Byrnes

- *Big Rock Candy Mountain,* by Wallace Stegner

- *Foreign Correspondence,* by Geraldine Brooks, author of *Nine Parts of Desire* (Anchor Australia, 1998)

- *If You Can Walk, You Can Dance,* by Marion Molento (Shola Books, 1998)

- *Like Water in Wild Places,* by Pamela Jooste (Doubleday, 2000)

- *Madame Sarah*, a biography of French actress Sarah Bernhardt, by Cornelia Otis Skinner

- *One More Time: A Memoir,* by Carol Burnett (Random House, 1986)

- *Poisonwood Bible,* by Barbara Kingsolver (Harperflamingo, 1999)

- *The Spy Wore Red*, by Aline, Countess of Romanones (reprint edition, Charter Books, 1990)

MOVIES

- *A League of Their Own*

- *Dolores Claiborne*

- *Erin Brokovich*

- *Evita*

- *Fried Green Tomatoes*

♦ *Gone with the Wind*

♦ *Mary Poppins*

♦ *Norma Rae*

♦ *Out of Africa*

♦ *Places in the Heart*

♦ *Shining Through*

♦ *Thelma and Louise*

♦ *Yentl*

PLAYS

♦ *Pygmalion,* by George Bernard Shaw, adapted by Alan Jay Lerner into the musical, *My Fair Lady*

♦ *The Matchmaker,* by Thornton Wilder, which he rewrote from his original version, *The Merchant of Yonkers,* which Jerry Herman adapted into the musical, *Hello Dolly*

SONGS

♦ "Feeling Good" as sung by Nina Simone, from her album, *Essential*

♦ "Happy Talk" from the musical *South Pacific*

Dianne Lorang and Ann E. Byrnes

- "I've Never Been To Me" as sung by Charlene

- "My Way" as sung by Frank Sinatra

- "That Was Yesterday" as sung by Wynonna, from her CD,

  Tell Me Why

- "Woman" as sung by Peggy Lee

TRAVEL

- AdventureWomen, 15033 Kelly Canyon Road, Bozeman, MT 59715;

  Toll-free: 1-800-804-8686; (406) 587-3883; www.adventurewomen.com

- Becoming an Outdoors-Woman, Colorado, (303) 291-7303;

  www.uwsp.edu/cnr/bow

- Elderhostel, 75 Federal Street, Boston, MA 02110; Toll-free:

  1-877-426-8056; www.elderhostel.org

- Gunflint Lodge, 143 S. Gunflint Lake, Grand Marais, MN 55604;

  Toll-free: 1-800-328-3325; (218) 388-2294; www.gunflint.com

- WomanTours, P.O. Box 68, Coleman Falls, VA 24536; Toll-free:

  1-800-247-1444; www.womantours.com

TRAVEL BOOKS (from Travelers' Tales Books, www.travelerstales.com)

♦ *A Mother's World*, edited by Marybeth Bond and Pamela Michael

♦ *A Woman's Passion for Travel*, edited by Marybeth Bond and Pamela Michael

♦ *A Woman's Path*, edited by Lucy McCauley, Amy G. Carson, and Jennifer Leo

♦ *A Woman's World,* edited by Marybeth Bond, introduction by Dervla Murphy

♦ *Gutsy Women,* by Marybeth Bond

♦ *Gutsy Mamas,* by Marybeth Bond

♦ *Safety and Security for Women Who Travel*, edited by Sheila Swan and Peter Laufer

♦ *Women in the Wild,* edited by Lucy McCauley

TV SHOWS

♦ *Judging Amy*

♦ *Star Trek Voyageur*

♦ *The Mary Tyler Moore Show*

♦ *The X-Files*

Index

www.ingramcontent.com/pod-product-compliance
Lightning Source LLC
Chambersburg PA
CBHW020420290526
45785CB00002B/659